SIZZLING QUILTS

from a

SIMPLE BLOCK

~ ANITA HALLOCK ~

Published by

krause publications

700 East State Street • Iola, WI 54990-0001
715/445-2214 • FAX: 715/445-4087   www.krause.com

Please call or write for our free catalog of publications. Our toll-free number to place an order or obtain a free catalog is 800-258-0929 or please use our regular business telephone 715-445-2214 for editorial comment and further information.

Library of Congress Catalog Number 99-61450
ISBN 0-87341-727-5

Illustrations by Anita Hallock
Photography by Walt Biddle
Back cover photography by Kris Kandler

**To my husband George and to Betsy,
our favorite Test Pilot.**

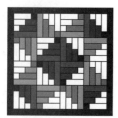

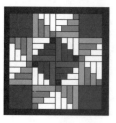

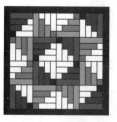

Table of Contents

Projects in This Book 6
Introduction 7
    How to Use This Book 7
    Thanks, Test Pilots! 8
How to Make Woodpile Block 9
    Tools and Supplies 10
    Fabric 10
    Mock-up Blocks 12
    Cutting Strategy 13
    Making Blocks 14
    Trimming Blocks 15
    Assembling the Quilt Top 16

Part 1 Regular Blocks 17
Choosing Fabrics 18
How a Typical Quilt is Made 19
Basic Ways to Arrange Blocks 20
Projects in the Most Popular Size 22
    1 Super Sixteen 22
    2 Marcella's Quilt 23
    3 Rain Dance 24
    4 Christmas Table Runner 25
Projects in Other Sizes and Steps 26
    5 Card Trick 27
    6 Betsy's Pinwheels 29
    7 Seven Stars 30
    8 Warm Hearts 31
Scrap Quilts 32
    9 Log Cabin Look-alike 33
    10 Kelly's Sweetheart Quilt 34
Stitch and Flip Triangles 35
    11 Fancy Paths 36
    12 Toasted Triangles 38
    13 Housewarming 39
    14 Glowing Pinwheels 40
"Anita's Sketchbook" Small Quilts 41
    Overall Arrangements for Almost Any Quilt 42
    Arrangements with Circle Centers 44
    Arrangements with Pinwheels Centers 48
Projects 1 to 4 Continued 55
Table Runners with 24 Blocks 59
"Design-Your-Own" Charts
    Three Steps 61
    Four Steps 62
    Five Steps 63
    Six Steps 64
    Total Length of Strips Needed 65

Projects 5 to 8 Continued 66
"Anita's Sketchbook" Large Quilts 71
Projects 9 to 14 Continued 77
"Design-Your-Own" Stitch and Flip Charts 87
Three Steps 87
Four Steps 88

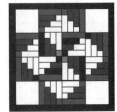

Part 2 Reverse Blocks 89
How to Make Reverse Blocks 90
Double Your Designs 91
15 Kachina 91
How to Arrange a Straight Furrows Design 93
16 Rainbow Hearts 94
How to Arrange a Barn-Raising Design 95
17 Barn Raising 96
Adventures with 100 Blocks 97
18 Before and After 98
More Design Ideas for Reverse Blocks 99
19 Cozy Quilt 101
20 Boca Barn Raising 102
21 Pinwheel Stars 103
22 Tulips in the Woodpile 104
Borders from Double Blocks 105
23 Fireman's Fancy 106
Making Shattered Blocks 108
24 Fanning the Fire 109
25 Irish Cabin 110
"Anita's Sketchbook" Review 113
Overall Patterns 114
Projects 15 to 18 Continued 116
"Anita's Sketchbook" 123
Arrangements with H/V Centers 123
Arrangements with V/H Centers 127
Summary of Design Ideas 131
More Ideas 132
Projects 19 to 25 Continued 136
Appendix 145
An Illustrative Glossary 145
Coloring Sheets for Design-Your-Own Quilts 146
Sizes and Number of Steps in the Projects 147
"Lemonade" 148
Calculating Curves 150
Help for Teachers 151
Mock-up Blocks 154
Quilts on the Covers 156
Related Books 157
Information on the Web 157
Index 158

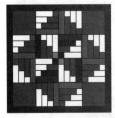

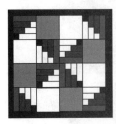

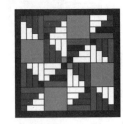

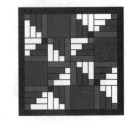

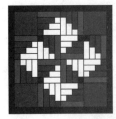

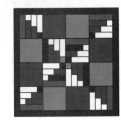

Projects in This Book

(Ranked by size and difficulty)

Categories are arranged by size. The projects listed first in each category are the easiest.

Small Wall Hangings
1 Super Sixteen 22
7 Seven Stars 30
11 Fancy Paths 36
25 Irish Cabin 110

Table Runners
4 Christmas Table Runner 25

Larger Wall Hangings and Baby Quilts
15 Kachina 91
3 Rain Dance 23
5 Card Trick 27
6 Betsy's Pinwheels 29
19 Cozy Quilt 101
2 Marcella's Quilt 23
16 Rainbow Hearts 94
13 Housewarming 39

Medium Quilts and Lap Robes
15 Kachina 91
21 Pinwheel Stars 103
20 Boca Barn Raising 102
12 Toasted Triangles 38
24 Fanning the Fire 109

Large Quilts
23 Fireman's Fancy 106
9 Log Cabin Look-alike 33
17 Barn Raising 96
10 Kelly's Sweetheart Quilt 34
8 Warm Hearts 31
18 Before and After 98
22 Tulips in the Woodpile 104
14 Glowing Pinwheels 40

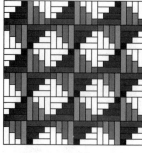

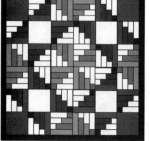

See page 147 for projects listed by block size and number of steps.

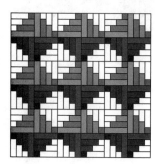

Introduction

The "Simple Block" in this book is one I call Woodpile. It's sort of a combination of Log Cabin and Rail Fence, so I gave it a woodsy name.

At a quilt show in 1990, I spotted a complicated quilt called Irish Cabin, made by seven friends in the San Francisco area. It wasn't strip pieced, but it could have been, so I borrowed it to photograph for my book on strip-pieced quilts, *Scrap Quilts Using Fast Patch* (see page 108). That quilt gave me the idea for a much simpler block, which I called Woodpile and used in the Log Cabin chapter. I simplified the block further for this book, then explored the ways to embellish the block and vary the arrangements so most of the projects no longer resemble Log Cabin.

How to Use This Book

Pick the Right Project

On the opposite page there is a list of the projects, arranged by size. Within each category the projects are arranged from easy to challenging. Pick something the right size and difficulty for your skill and time.

If you don't have a preference, start with Project 1, Super Sixteen. After making your blocks and playing with arrangements, all of the other ideas in the book will make more sense. If you don't have a need for a small wall hanging, use those 16 blocks as the start of a larger project.

Start with Color Pages, Continue in Black and White Pages

We tried to give you just the right balance of color and black and white pages. We show all 25 projects in color, along with a lot of other colored art and photographs. To give you a nice thick book at a reasonable cost, we use black and white pages otherwise—a whole lot of them to hold all the charts and design ideas. Each project begins in color, then is continued in the black and white section. Use a bit of the money you saved to buy Post-it Notes or paper clips to mark pages and make it easy to flip back and forth between the beginning of the project and the end.

Getting Out of Trouble

No matter how carefully you choose your fabric, when you get your blocks made and lay them out, you sometimes just don't like the effect as much as you thought you would. Now is where the real adventure begins. Fixing something that doesn't work is what gives creative, new ideas their start. (Plus researchers have found that solving puzzles keeps your mind healthy.) I have dozens of pages called "Anita's Sketchbook" which show a wide variety of ways to arrange blocks. Try several small designs from page 48, using plain blocks to separate fighting color and enlarge the quilt. Add striped inserts on one side of some blocks as shown in Project 3. Add a border of blocks from page 49. Try this layout and that, and this border and that.

If you are doing Projects 1 to 14, stick to the Sketchbooks in the first half of the book. For Projects 15 to 23, use Sketchbooks in the second half.

Designing a Quilt from Scratch

Although you can copy our color schemes and arrangements, you don't need to. You can use them only for ideas, but use the "Design Your Own" and "Sketchbook" pages to plan projects from scratch. Find an arrangement, determine how many strips you need from each color scheme, and find the length of the strips on page 65. If necessary, locate a project with the same size and scale of blocks and follow the step-by-step directions for that project.

The element of mystery when you start ("What will my blocks look like?"), and maybe some anxiety when you get partway done ("Have I ruined my beautiful fabric?"), and the pride when you solve your problems and create something unique are all parts of the appeal of quiltmaking.

Have fun and make something great!

Thanks, Test Pilots!

When I signed the contract to do this book, I thought, "How can I fill up 160 pages with one simple block? Will I have enough material?"

Then I started sewing, playing with ideas on the computer, and discussing ideas with guests at our Fast Patch quilt retreats. When word got around that a book was in the works, I started getting snapshots of projects other people had made. Eventually, I decided I had way too many ideas for one book and should divide the material into two books.

Then I thought, "When will I learn not to torture myself so much? Writing books is hard work! I'll finish this one, cramming in every idea that fits, and never write another one!"

Meanwhile, several friends I had met in classes and retreats said they'd be willing to make some of the samples. (I call these wonderful people "Test Pilots," because it sounds better than "guinea pigs.") I appreci-ated their offers, but I couldn't send them instructions until I decided which projects to include. Finally, a few weeks before my deadline, I made some decisions and sent off a few final projects to try. The Test Pilots came through in great style, considering some of them had only a few days. They didn't have time to quilt the projects, but they did a wonderful job rushing the quilt tops to me. I appreciate them so much!

(Will there be another Woodpile book? I don't know. Writing books is somewhat like having babies. You forget the pain and are eager to do it again in a few years.)

I hope you enjoy this book as much as I will think I enjoyed writing it when I look back years from now.

Anita Hallock
Springfield, Oregon

How to Make Woodpile Blocks

I love the Woodpile block. The basic idea is so simple! Just cut long strips and piece them together…

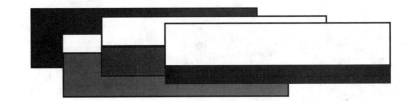

Cut cross-sections…

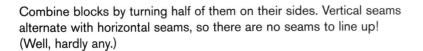

And sew sections to each other, progressing gradually from dark on one side to light on the other. At one end there will be a solid dark or light strip.

Combine blocks by turning half of them on their sides. Vertical seams alternate with horizontal seams, so there are no seams to line up! (Well, hardly any.)

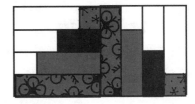

The sections form "steps." Blocks can have as few as two steps or as many as six. They can be made on a large or small scale just by varying the size of the strips and cross-sections.

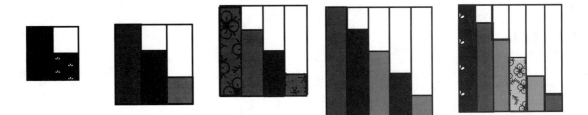

The next few pages will give details about how to make the blocks. The rest of the book gives many ways the blocks can be varied and dozens of interesting ways to arrange the finished blocks.

Tools and Supplies

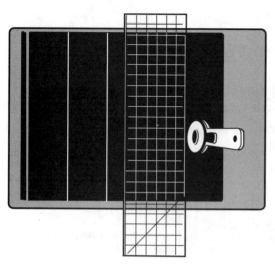

The tools used for strip-piecing are pretty standard with quiltmakers now:

Rotary cutter

Cutting mats. Have a big one (at least 18" x 24"), plus a small mat/pressing board combination right by your sewing machine, if possible.

6" x 24" ruler

Square grids, at least as large as the quilt blocks you are making (6" to 9-1/2") to square up the blocks.

Iron and ironing board

Sewing machine. All piecing is done by machine (and quilting can be also).

Thread. Unless there is a dominant color, just use neutral gray or brown thread for the whole quilt top. Use matching thread or metallic thread for machine quilting.

Standard sewing supplies (pins, seam ripper, etc.)

Glue Stick, pencil, paper, etc. for planning and making mock-up blocks.

Reducing glass for viewing quilt design (can substitute camera lens or peephole; see page 145)

How About a Serger?

If you like to use a serger, by all means use it for the first sewing step, sewing strips in pairs. That's when you appreciate the speed, and when seam width isn't critical. Use the serger for the whole quilt, if you wish, but I don't have directions geared for that.

Fabric

Use 100" cotton as a rule. Simple large-scale blocks might be made from heavy fabrics.

Good:

Small prints

Small-scale plaids

Solid colors (especially for the A strips)

Variegated, hand-dyed fabrics

Do not use:

Large prints with high figure/background contrast

Be careful with:

Medium-size prints; they are best used for the end strips (see page 18)

Stripes and directional fabrics; they can look striking, but you might need more fabric so you can cut strips so the stripes run the right way (see page 13).

Usually best for the design: **Usually not desirable:**

Selvage

More About Fabrics

Choose Between Warm and Cool

Use basically warm with cool accents or use basically cool colors with warm accents.

Think About Lights and Darks

It's usually best to use a fairly high contrast between dark and light and to avoid medium fabrics; however, you can have a pastel quilt where medium is "dark" or a dark quilt where medium is "light." The lightest light is usually best in the smallest squares; I often use pure white. The darkest dark often goes in the smallest dark squares too, but if you have more than one color scheme, it's more important to have contrast among those small dark squares, because they often touch in the quilt layout.

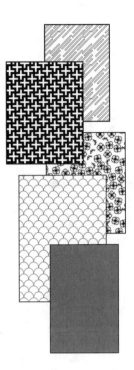

Let the Experts Help You

If you have no confidence with colors, there's lots of help available. Go to your favorite quilt shop and select from its color-coordinated displays and packets of fat quarters. Copy the color scheme of a prize-winning quilt (but don't try to copy the exact fabrics), or choose a colorful fabric designed by professionals and copy the colors in it.

Decide How Many Different Color Schemes to Use

Projects 1, 6, 7, 11, 12, 13, 16, and 25 have the same fabrics in all blocks, but most Woodpile quilts have two or more basic color schemes arranged creatively.

The effect is richer if you have variety **within** each color scheme. Project 21 is a real scrap quilt with two distinct color schemes, for example. Other times you plan to make a small quilt and decide to make it larger but can't find any more of the fabrics used earlier. Don't worry. The quilt will probably be more interesting with some new fabrics in the same general color schemes.

If you repeat fabrics in different sets, do it in the inner parts (Light A and B, Dark B and C in the diagram). Use as big a variety as possible in the end pieces (Dark A and D, Light C).

See pages 16 and 18 for more information on color strategy.

Make a Mock-up Block for Each Color Scheme

It is really helpful with most projects to make mock-up blocks with actual fabric pieces pasted up. Not only do they help you work up your color scheme, but they are a guide to cutting and sewing strips.

See page 12 for diagrams for three, four, five, and six steps. If you are a teacher (or just want a lot of copies of four-step diagrams), see pages 154 and 155.

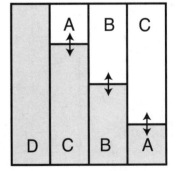

Mock-up Blocks

Make photocopies of this sheet. Study the color tips on page 18 and cut 1/2" snippits of fabric you are thinking of using for each block. Tape or paste them onto the paper as a guide. I give two copies of most sizes, because you often use at least two color schemes.

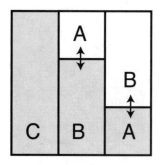

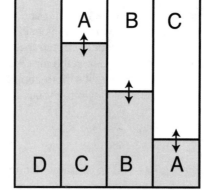

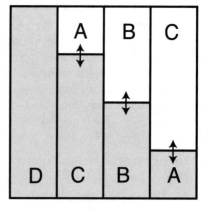

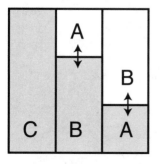

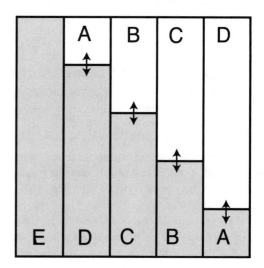

I usually use six steps (below) for scrap quilts, which don't need mock-up blocks.

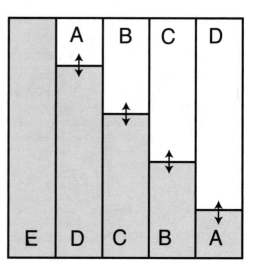

Cutting Strategy

Here are guidelines for cutting strips for most projects. See page 75 if you are making scrap quilts.

1. Cut strips which will be pieced. Check your mock-up blocks and choose all A fabrics. They are all the same width, so cut them at the same time, if you wish. Repeat with all B fabrics, C fabrics, etc. Just spread out as many layers as is convenient, trim one edge, and cut strips.

Caution: If using folded fabric, make sure your fabric and ruler are square with each other so the strips don't change angles at the fold. If they bend, you might want to cut them at that point and work with shorter strips.

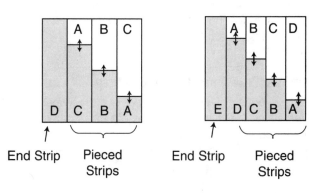

End Strip Pieced Strips   End Strip Pieced Strips

2. Cut end strips. The long strips on the edge of the block are solid, not pieced. There are two ways to cut them:

a. Cut a wide panel (the length of the end strip) to cut into sections later. Do it this way if...

> You're making blocks with two, four, or six steps (strips are paired with a pieced panel to cut sections)... or
> The design goes this way... or
> The math works out best.

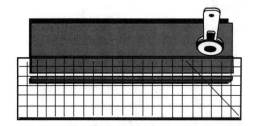

b. Cut narrow strips (the width of the end strips) to cut into lengths later. Do it this way if...

> You're making three- or five-step blocks (strips aren't paired with pieced panels for cutting cross-sections)... or
> You're making a scrap quilt and want a big variety... or
> The design goes this way... or
> The math works out best.

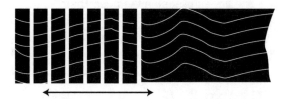

Making end strips from long narrow strips–does the math work?
Number of end strips you can cut from 44" lengths:

	Mini	Small	Normal	Large
Three steps	2-3/4"	3-1/2"	4-1/4"	5"
	15 strips	12 strips	10 strips	8 strips
Four steps	4"	5"	6"	7"
	10 or 11 strips	8 strips	7 strips	6 strips
Five steps	4-3/4"	6"	7-1/4"	8-1/2"
	9 strips	7 strips	5 or 6 strips	5 strips
Six steps	5-1/2"	7"	8-1/2"	10"
	7 or 8 strips	6 strips	5 strips	4 strips

Using Fat Quarters?

If the chart shows an even number of strips, you can cut half this many from 22" strips, of course.

If the math (or design of the fabric) works better, cut the other direction, making 18" lengths.

Making Blocks

1. Sew Strips in Pairs

Use 1/4" seams, about 12 stitches to the inch. If you find any strips bent at the fold, cut them apart at that point. Cut strips you will sew together to the same lengths, or just butt shorter strips against each other like this: Press toward the darker color.

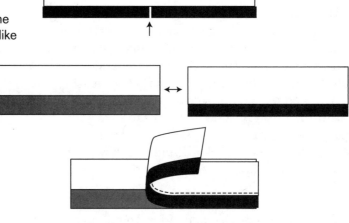

2. Lay Out Panels for Cutting

In project directions, you will see diagrams something like this. Carefully lay out these panels together, right sides together, dark edges together closest to you, larger light section on top layer.

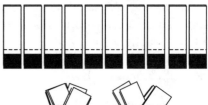

3. Cut Sections

Cut cross-sections as directed, from 1-1/4" wide for mini to 2" for large scale. Can't cut all of the sections you need? Cut a few loose pieces and sew them together.

Craftsmanship tip: As you cut, make sure seams line up with lines on the ruler. There's no need to discard slightly slanted sections, but if you notice a problem, square up the ends and continue more accurately.

If panels are aligned correctly, these sections will be lined up ready to sew. Stack cross-sections like this, the sections with the most light fabric still on top.

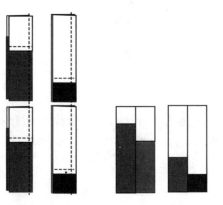

4. Sew Cross-sections Together

- Sew with a scant 1/4" seam.
- Chain sections like this for efficiency.
- Back stitch 1/4" from the ends because the ends will usually be trimmed off.
- Keep largest light section on top, and when you open up the sections, they will look like this:

5. Make a Test Block

Sew the parts together (light still on top). Add an end strip if you are making a block with five steps. When you open up the block, the steps will go down (reading left to right). Check the test block to make sure the width is accurate before making all blocks.

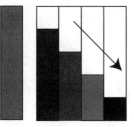

6. Check the Test Block for Accuracy and Trim It

Press this first block and trim it. The blocks need to be square, and all measurements shown in brackets should be the same so seams will line up when the blocks are sewn to each other.

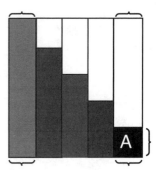

In most projects, there's an allowance of 1/4" at the top and bottom of the block for squaring it up.

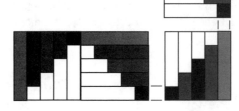

a)
1. Trim the small square first.
Place your grid over the block with numbers 1-2-3 at the small square. Cover this much of that square (piece A):

> Mini blocks: 1"
> Small blocks: 1-1/4"
> Normal blocks: 1-1/2"
> Large blocks: 1-3/4"

Trim that end. (Avoid trimming the side.)

b)
2. Rotate the block
Adjust the grid so it covers a block as long as it is wide. Edges of the block hit the same numbers on each side (6-3/4" for a Normal block with five steps). Trim about 1/4" from that end.

> If the block is too wide, widen one or two seams a bit.
> If block is too narrow, pick out a seam and sew a narrower one.

Adjust future seam widths as necessary. These blocks go together fast if you can square the blocks up quickly.

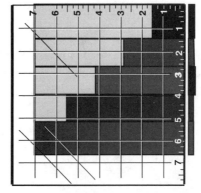

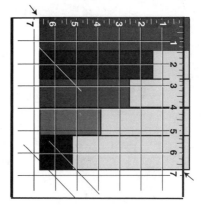

Other Accuracy Checks

The other A squares: These should be the same length as the corner ones, but 1/4" narrower because both side seams have been sewn.

The height of the step: If your cutting and sewing have been a little sloppy and sections aren't uniform, cut a cardboard guide to space the overlapping area as you sew. Cut it this wide:

> Mini blocks: 3/4"
> Small blocks: 1"
> Normal blocks: 1-1/4"
> Large blocks: 1-1/2"

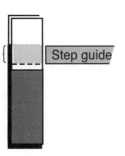

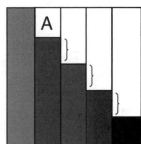

You can feel the seam in the bottom layer or see a shadow through the top fabric.

Assembling the Quilt Top

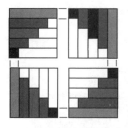

Watch the little Dark A squares

For most layouts, the small Dark A squares are crucial. Sometimes all of these squares must line up with seams of neighboring blocks. If you failed to square up those pieces first when trimming the blocks, I suggest you switch to another design! See the Appendix for a handy chart showing which projects are the most forgiving.

Usually not desirable: Better:

Avoid Big Dark Blobs

Try having a color contrast where small squares come together. Sometimes you can't avoid the same colors touching. See Betsy's Pinwheels, page 29. Also see Rain Dance, page 24, for striped inserts between the squares. Usually you can plan ahead and use contrasting Dark A colors when you plan your color schemes

Usually not desirable: Better:

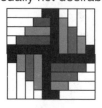

Avoid Swastikas

Swastika have long been a disturbing symbol most of us wouldn't deliberately use. Plan ahead so they don't occur accidentally: Don't have the same color for the dark A squares and the long dark end strips.

Usually not desirable: Better:

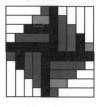

Avoid "Spines"

Sometimes in scrap quilts, an unpleasant look occurs when the same fabric is used for the dark end strips on one block and a perpendicular strip in the neighboring block. I have learned to use unique fabrics for the end strips, not using them in any other part of the quilt.

Usually not desirable: Better:

Avoid "Long Arms"

Try not to have the dark end strips meet a small square of the same color. If you use similar fabrics for end strips and A squares, it's bound to occur occasionally.

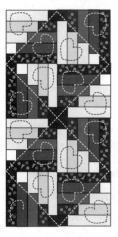

Borders

The rules are simple: Use whatever border colors and widths you wish. That's a creative decision I don't make until I can lay out the blocks to "audition" different fabrics. I give yardage for borders to match the photo, but you can ignore it.

Quilting and Binding

Unfortunately, I don't have room in this book for instructions on quilting and binding. There are many wonderful books available, and the folks at your favorite quilt shop offer classes and maybe some free advice (especially if you buy your supplies there).

One good solution: Have your project commercially quilted. Most projects in this book look fine with a quilting pattern that doesn't follow the patchwork design. Again, ask the staff at the quilt shop to recommend someone who does commercial quilting.

Part 1 • Regular Blocks

The first half of the book has a variety of projects with one thing in common, the blocks all slant like this:

Here Are a Few Examples:

Right: Blocks are tiny in this quilt, but the design goes together fast because of all of the plain blocks. Pam Mennis of Norwich, New York, made this version of Project 7, "Seven Stars."

Left: Ann Roland of Woodland, California, made this striking example of Stitch and Flip triangles. See Project 13 to make a similar quilt.

Below: Muriel Erlandson of Elk Grove, California, started making Project 1 but expanded it into this pretty 43" x 53" quilt.

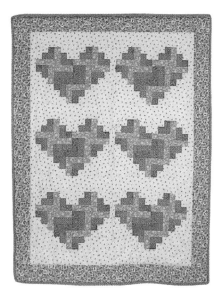

Above: Solid color pieced blocks can be worked into the design. My daughter, Betsy Heath of Cheshire, Massachusetts, made this as a smaller version of Project 10.

Choosing Fabrics

Your first step is usually to make one or more mock-up blocks. Fold and overlap fabrics to suggest a full-size block (dotted lines). Substitute new fabrics until you find a combination you like. Here are some proven guidelines.

1. Usually the lightest, maybe white. (Light A, B, C can all be the same.)

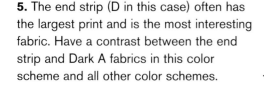

2. A subtle print or interesting texture is nice here.

5. The end strip (D in this case) often has the largest print and is the most interesting fabric. Have a contrast between the end strip and Dark A fabrics in this color scheme and all other color schemes.

3. Solid color or small print. Should contrast with Dark D. Using two or more color schemes? Try to have a contrast with **all** Dark A and Dark D fabrics.

4. Medium-size prints making a color transition between A and D. These can be repeated in same spot if you have several color schemes.

6. Making blocks with five or six steps? Rules for D would apply to whatever is on the end (E or F).

7. Making several color schemes? Rules for B and C would apply to all inner colors. It's okay to keep inner colors similar. Use some contrast among all the Dark A and end strips.

When you are happy with your folded-fabric decisions, make a mock-up block for every color scheme. Make photocopies of pages 12, 148, or 149, or just make sketches of the blocks. Use a glue stick or Scotch Tape to attach snippits of fabric right to the paper diagrams for a reference.

Do you have to follow all of the color rules? No, but you have a wider choice of arrangements if you do.

I made up kits for a class in Attleboro, Massachusetts, knowing that having the largest print on the end wasn't as important as having a nice transition between colors. I often have the small dark (A) squares a bright accent color. Black, being neutral, provided a transition between blue and red. Helen Carmichael made this table runner, at left. (To make a similar one, follow directions for Project 1, but make strips 44" long so you can make 24 blocks. Also see pages 59 and 60.)

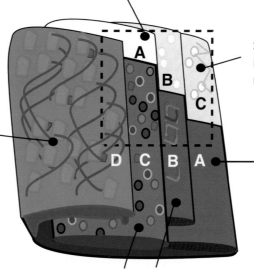

How a Typical Quilt Is Made

Right: Here's a quick photo guide to making Woodpile blocks. Please read pages 14 to 16 for details. The finished blocks are used for Project 3.

Above: Consulting the mock-up block, sew the fabrics together in pairs and press toward the darks. Notice that fabrics which will be sewn together are connected by an arrow in the mock-up block. One strip doesn't have a partner.

Above: Lay out the pairs of strips right sides together for cutting and you'll automatically have sections aligned ready to sew. Have the darker edges of both layers toward you and the largest light strips on top. Cut cross-sections the width given in the directions.

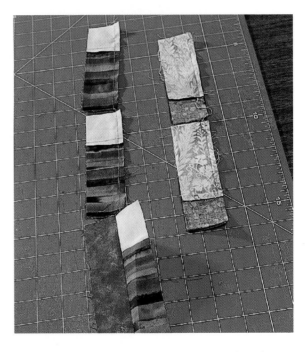

Above: Sew the sections together, keeping the largest light section on top and chaining for efficiency. Use scant 1/4" seams.

Join the pairs into a test block. Press it and measure to make sure it is the right width. Most projects give a 1/4" allowance for trimming the ends. Square up the block, starting with the Dark A square (see page 15). Once you know the exact seam width to use, the blocks go together fast.

Basic Ways to Arrange Blocks

Blocks are arranged with seams alternating vertical and horizontal and colors where they are needed for a pleasing design. Because most designs are built up from the center, study these four basic center arrangements:

Here is a 16-block design built up from a circle center (see Project 1, page 22).

Circle Centers

On the left, the dark colors form a circle. On the right, the lights make a smaller circle because there are fewer light fabrics. In an overall design, light and dark circles often alternate.

You'll see many more examples throughout the book, especially on pages 44 to 47.

This wall hanging by Marcella Monbaron of Sutherlin, Oregon, is based on Pinwheels. Four 16-block designs are combined into one large design. See the following pages for more Pinwheel ideas.

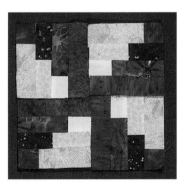 

Pinwheel Centers

Notice that the vertical/horizontal position of seams in Pinwheel arrangements is opposite from that used for circles.

The Pinwheel on the left has end strips meeting. The one on the right has four small squares meeting and it revolves the other direction. You can usually decide after blocks are made which way you want the block to revolve. Again, in an overall arrangement, the two types of Pinwheels might alternate.

This wall hanging Marcella Monbaron of Sutherlin, Oregon, is making is based on Pinwheels. Four 16-block designs are combined into one large design. See the following pages for more Pinwheel ideas.

Projects in the Most Popular Size
Project 1 • Super Sixteen

To get acquainted with a new technique, make 16 blocks for a wall hanging. (When these are assembled you might decide to make another set of 16 and add a border of blocks, as mentioned on page 55.) This quilt was made by Susan Zimlich of the Country Sewing Center in Elk Grove, California.

Quilt size: About 30" square
Block size: 5"
Total blocks: 16

Make a mock-up block (pages 12 and 18) to select fabrics.

Fabric

Single strips from scraps (See Step 1)
Narrow borders: 1/8 yard bright, 1/4 yard dark
Wide borders: 1/2 yard dark (use a strip for blocks too)
Lining: 1 yard (use a strip for blocks too)

1. Cut one strip of each size:

Dark fabrics	Light fabrics
A = 2" x 29"	2" x 29"
B = 3-1/4" x 29"	3-1/4" x 29"
C = 4-1/2" x 29"	4-1/2" x 29"
D = 6" x 29"	

(If using fat quarters, cut two strips 15" long of each)

2. Sew strips together in pairs. Sew each light strip to the dark partner below it on the mock-up block (D has no partner). Press toward the dark.

3. Lay out two panels at a time. Pair off as shown. Keep darks on the lower edges (toward you) and keep right sides together. See page 14.

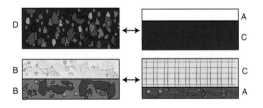

4. Cut each set into 1-3/4" cross-sections. Keep darks and lights in the position shown. Cut 16 sections from each combination and stack them like this:

5. Sew pairs together. Keeping the light sections on top, chain the pieces together. Use a scant 1/4" seam.
6. Make a test block. Sew sets into a block. Press and measure it; it should be 5-1/2" wide.
7. Complete 16 blocks. Adjust seam width as needed so all are 5-1/2" wide.
8. Square up blocks (see page 15). Trim blocks to 5-1/2" square with the small dark square 1-1/2" square.

(Project 1 continued on page 55)

Project 2 • Marcella's Quilt

Repeat a 16-block arrangement four times for this project, then make some creative changes, if needed, to improve the design. This quilt is by Marcella Monbaron of Sutherlin, Oregon.

Quilt size: About 50" square
Block size: 5"
Total blocks: 60 or 64

48 "reds"   12 or 16 "blues"

Fabric

21 strips, see Step 1
Inner borders: 1/3 yard
Outer borders: 2/3 yard
Lining: 2-1/2 yards

Make two mock up blocks (see pages 12 and 18).

1. Cut 21 strips. Cut **two** strips of each for "red" blocks.

Dark fabrics	Light fabrics
A = 2" x 44"	2" x 44"
B = 3-1/4" x 44"	3-1/4" x 44"
C = 4-1/2" x 44"	4-1/2" x 44"
D = 6" x 44"	

Cut one strip of each for "blue" blocks.

Dark fabrics	Light fabrics
A = 2" x 29"	2" x 29"
B = 3-1/4" x 29"	3-1/4" x 29"
C = 4-1/2" x 29"	4-1/2" x 29"
D = 6" x 29"	

(If you want only 12 blocks, use 22" strips.)

2. Sew strips for "red" blocks. Sew each light to a dark partner. Press toward the darks.

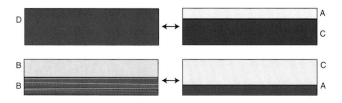

Tip: If using striped fabric, have it go the directions shown above.

3. Lay out two panels at a time. Pair off, right sides together, so cross-sections will be lined up ready to sew. See page 14.
4. Cut each set into 1-3/4" cross-sections. Keep darks and lights in the position shown. Cut 24 sections from each combination. Stack them like this:

Tip: If you can't cut all of the cross-sections you need in Step 4, just cut a few individual pieces for the last block.

5. Sew pairs together. Use a scant 1/4" seam.
6. Make a test block. Press and measure it; it should be 5-1/2" wide.

(Project 2 continued on page 56)

Project 3 • Rain Dance

When I made this quilt with Southwestern colors, I decided to separate the touching squares in the center with striped inserts, and I really liked the effect. Take your time choosing just the right fabrics, especially the striped fabric. (In a hurry? Omit the stripes. Using plain blocks makes this a speedy quilt if you don't fuss with creative touches.)

Quilt size: About 41" x 51" with borders
Block size: 5"
Total blocks: 24; eight each of three different color schemes.

Make three mock-up blocks to select fabrics (see pages 12 and 18).

Fabric

Single strips of about 15 fabrics (see Step 1 and the box below)
Accent strips: 1/4 yard of two striped fabrics (optional)
Plain blocks: 2/3 yard light
Inner border: 1/3 yard
Outer border: 1/2 yard or more
Lining: 1-1/2 yards

Choosing Fabrics

Stripes: For blocks, cut **with** the stripes. For borders, you'll cut **across** the stripes, so allow enough fabric to have minimum piecing.
Dark fabrics: You can repeat any fabrics in the same place in two color schemes.
Light fabrics: It's okay to use only three, in the same place in all blocks. Cut 44" strips of each, then cut into three lengths. I suggest:
  Light A: Pure white
  Light B: The background fabric (see the cutting layout on page 57; cut along selvage).
  Light C: A large, pale print
You can even use just one light fabric for both the blocks and background (increase it to 1 yard).

1. Cut 21 strips. Cut three strips of each size, one for each color course (match the mock-up blocks):

Dark fabrics	Light fabrics
A = 2" x 15"	2" x 15"
B = 3-1/4" x 15"	3-1/4" x 15"
C = 4-1/2" x 15"	4-1/2" x 15"
D = 6" x 15"	

(These can be as short as 14-1/4", if you cut cross-sections very carefully.)

2. Sew one set of strips together. Use the mock-up block as a guide. Press toward the dark.
3. Lay out two panels at a time. Pair off, right sides together, largest light area on top, so you can cut cross-sections which are lined up ready to sew.

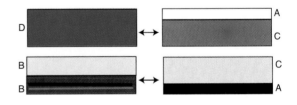

4. Cut 1-3/4" cross-sections. Cut eight sections from each combination. Stack them like this:

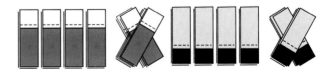

(Project 3 continued on page 57)

Project 4 • Christmas Table Runner

These blocks have accent squares down the center. This sample by Nancy Foisy of Coos Bay, Oregon, has lamé and elegant Christmas fabrics. Add metallic trim, beads, or fringes if desired.

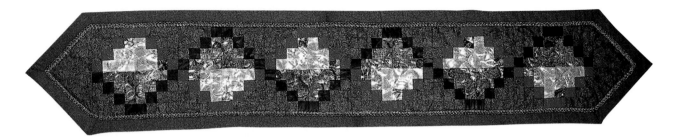

Project size: 14" x 72"
Block size: 5"
Total blocks: 24

Make 12 of each:

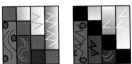

Make two mock-up blocks. Sketch your own diagrams. Paste up snippets, including red or black squares.

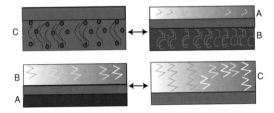

Fabric and Trim

One fat quarter of each:
    Gold lamé
    Silver lamé
    Red (polished cotton is nice)
    Black (ditto)
    Green or multicolor metallic Christmas print
Alternate: Use scraps of many different fabrics; see Step 1.
Border and lining: 1 yard green or dark blue
Optional: 4 yards gold metallic trim

1. Cut 20 strips. Stack and cut through several layers at a time:
a. Four red strips 1-3/4" x 22".
b. Four black strips 1-3/4" x 22".
c. Two green strips of each size:
    A = 2" x 22"
    B = 3-1/4" x 22"
    C = 4-1/2" x 22"
d. One gold strip of each of the above sizes (2", 3-1/4", and 4-1/2").
e. One silver strip of each size (2", 3-1/4", and 4-1/2").
2. Sew the first set of strips together.
a. Following the mock-up blocks, sew each silver strip to a red strip, then to the green below. (One set has no green and one has no silver.)
b. Press all toward the red.

3. Lay out two panels at a time. Pair off, right sides together, to cut cross-sections. Make sure the bottom edge of the red in one layer is aligned with the top edge of the red in the other layer.

4. Cut each set into 1-3/4" cross-sections. Keep colors in the position shown. You'll get 12 sections from each combination. Stack them like this:

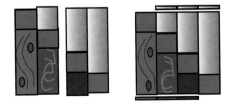

5. Sew pairs together. Chain for sewing. Use a scant 1/4" seam. Make sure seams of red fabric are lined up neatly; ends will be uneven.
6. Make a test block. Sew sets into a block. Press and measure it; it should be 5-1/2" wide. Trim ends to square up the block. Don't trim the red.

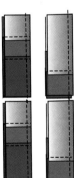

(Project 4 continued on page 58)

Sizzling 25 Quilts

Projects in Other Sizes and Steps

The first few projects used 5" blocks, with four steps taking you from solid dark to one little square of dark. There are many other sizes of blocks you can make.

You can vary the number of steps. For example:
Two Steps (Card Trick, Project 4)
Three steps (Kelly's Sweetheart Quilt, Project 10)
Five steps (Betsy's Pinwheels, Project 6)
Six steps (Log Cabin Look-alike, Project 9)

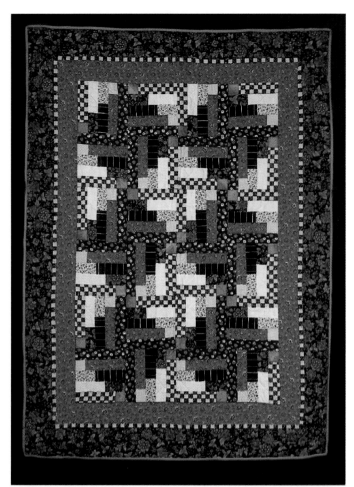

And you can vary the scale. The scale is determined by the width of the cross-sections cut.
Mini: 1-1/4" sections, 3/4" after seams
Small: 1-1/2" sections, 1" after seams
Normal: 1-3/4" sections, 1-1/4" after seams
Large: 2" sections, 1-1/2" after seams

On page 147, in the Appendix, there is a list of projects in each size. Like to design your own unique quilts? Use the "Design-Your-Own" charts on pages 61 to 64 plan projects in any of these sizes.

My Christmas quilt, at right, uses five steps, Normal scale.

My colorful scrap quilts, below, have five steps, Small scale.

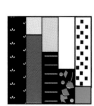

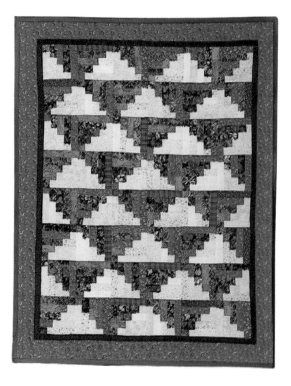

Project 5 • Card Trick

The simplest block has just two steps. What makes the project interesting is how four blocks are combined to make a traditional old quilt pattern, Card Trick.

Quilt size: About 34" x 42" before borders, about 44" x 52" after borders
Block size: 3" (Four blocks combined: 6")
Large scale, two steps
Make 80 blocks; 20 of each of these color schemes:

Fabric

Green: 3/4 yard (blocks plus border)
Brown: 1/2 yard (blocks plus border)
Blue: 1/4 yard
Red: 1/4 yard
Background: 1-1/8 yard
Lining: 1-1/2 yards

1. Cut strips. From each bright color:
  One strip 2" x 44"
  One strip 3-3/4" x 44"
From background color:
  Four strips 2" x 44"
2. Sew each narrow bright strip to a background strip. Use 1/4" seams. Press toward the darker color.
3. Arrange strips in pairs for cutting sections. Double-check to make sure colors are paired off like this:

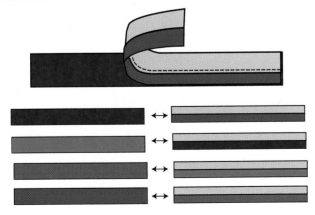

4. Cut through both layers into 2" sections. Stack pairs, ready to sew without fur-

ther alignment. Repeat with all color combinations.
5. Sew pairs together. Press toward the dark.

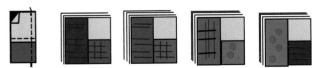

6. Sew two blocks together. Make sure colors are in this position. (Notice the Blue and Brown "7"s?)

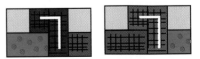

Press toward the longer pieces.

(Project 5 continued on page 66)

Alternatives to Card Tricks

Cut the same number of strips as in Card Tricks, Project 5, but change colors and arrangements for a very different look.

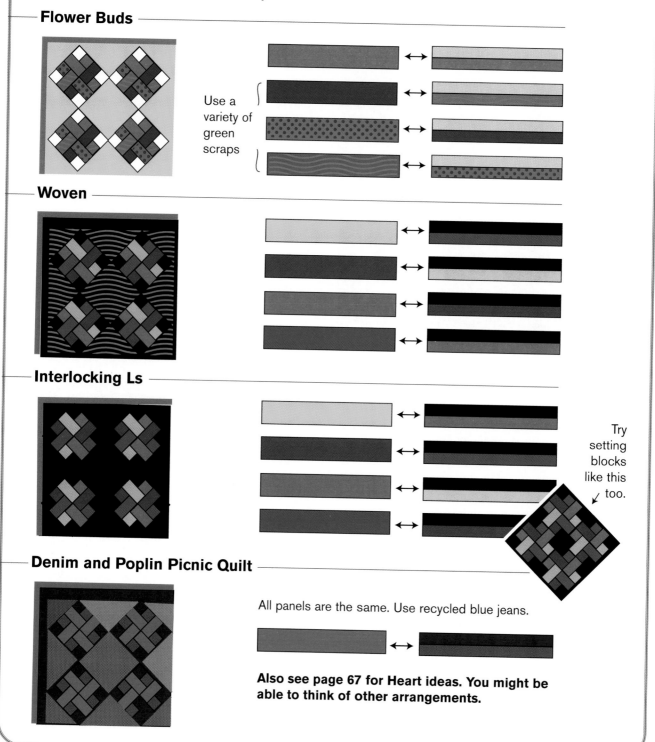

Flower Buds

Use a variety of green scraps

Woven

Interlocking Ls

Try setting blocks like this too.

Denim and Poplin Picnic Quilt

All panels are the same. Use recycled blue jeans.

Also see page 67 for Heart ideas. You might be able to think of other arrangements.

Project 6 • Betsy's Pinwheels

This crib quilt, made by my daughter, Betsy Heath of Cheshire, Massachusetts, has alternating Pinwheels. This overall pattern can be used for virtually any size of quilt.

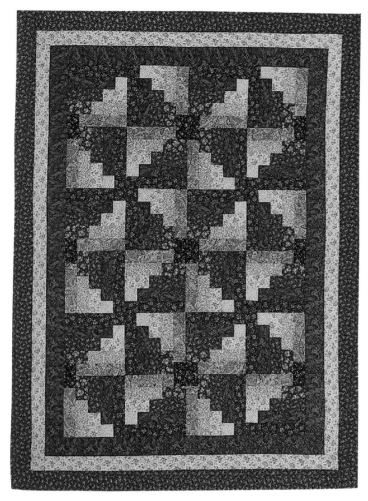

Quilt size: 38" x 52"
Block size: 6-1/4" square
Normal scale, five steps
Total blocks: 24

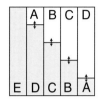

Make a mock-up block to choose fabric (see pages 12 and 18).

Fabric

Dark fabrics	Light fabrics
A = 1/8 yard	1/8 yard
B = 1/8 yard	1/2 yard*
C = 2/3 yard*	1/4 yard
D = 2/3 yard*	1/4 yard
E = 1/3 yard	

Lining: 1-1/2 yards
*Includes borders

1. Cut one strip of each fabric

Dark fabrics	Light fabrics
A = 2" x 44"	2" x 44"
B = 3-1/4" x 44"	3-1/4" x 44"
C = 4-1/2" x 44"	4-1/2" x 44"
D = 5-3/4" x 44"	5-3/4" x 44"
E = 7-1/4" x 44"	

2. Sew strips together. Follow the mock-up block. Press toward the dark.

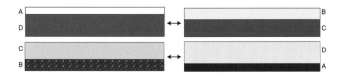

3. Arrange in pairs for cutting cross-sections. Keep darks on the lower edges and keep right sides together.

4. Cut 1-3/4" cross-sections. Cut 24 sections from the E strip and pieced sets. Keep darks and lights in this position. Stack them as shown. If you can't cut 24 cross-sections, cut a few individual pieces from remnants and piece them together.

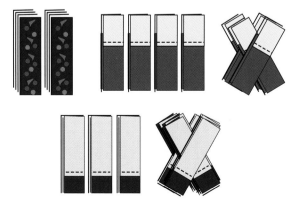

(Project 6 continued on page 68)

Project 7 • Seven Stars

I made this perky little wall hanging to experiment with miniature blocks. Lots of solid blocks make the 28 Woodpile blocks go a long way.

Quilt size: About 29" square after borders
Block size: 3" square
Mini blocks, four steps
Total blocks: 28

Make a mock-up block to choose fabric (see pages 12 and 18).

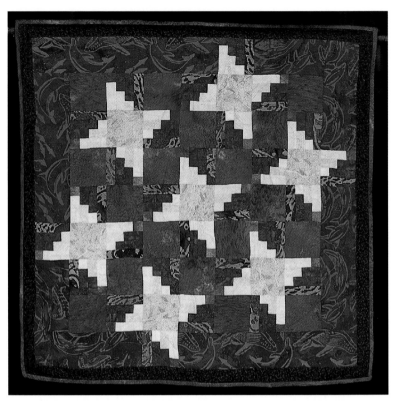

Fabric

Dark fabrics	Light fabrics
A = 1/8 yard	1/8 yard
B = 1/8 yard	1/8 yard
C = 1/8 yard	1/8 yard
D = 1/8 yard	

Plain blocks: 1/8 yard Light
Plain blocks: 1/4 yard Dark
Wide borders: 1/3 yard
Narrow borders: 1/4 yard
Lining: Piece about 31" square

Scraps or fat quarters can be used for any of these. Even fat eighths (11" x 18") will work in most cases.

1. Cut strips, referring to mock-up blocks:

Dark fabrics	Light fabrics
A = 1-1/2" x 38"	1-1/2" x 38"
B = 2-1/4" x 38"	2-1/4" x 38"
C = 3" x 38"	3" x 38"
D = 4" x 38"	

> Alternate ways to cut strips: Using fat quarters? Cut two 19" strips of each. Using fat eighths? Cut two 18" strips. If you run short in Step 4, cut a few individual pieces.

2. Sew strips together.
3. Arrange panels for cutting. Keep right sides together so cross-sections are aligned for sewing.

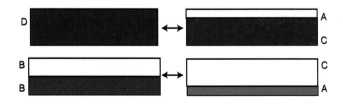

4. Cut 1-1/4" cross-sections. Stack with the largest light sections on top. You need 28 of each type.

5. Assemble 28 blocks. Make a test block first (see pages 14 and 15). Trim and square up the blocks. They should be 3-1/2" square. If they're a bit smaller, that's okay, as long as they are uniform.

(Project 7 continued on page 69)

Project 8 • Warm Hearts

I sent this project to Laura Rohwedder of Newark, California, suggesting closely related colors. She chose to use bright colors and changed the design a bit, inventing the heart pattern along the edges and breaking the rules in the corners. Remember it's your project and you too can make creative changes! Laura used 36 or 40 blocks of three different colors; the math works better for five color schemes, 24 blocks of each, so I'll give calculations for that.

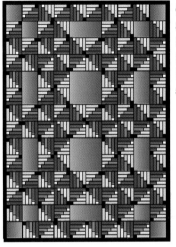

Quilt size: 63" x 88"
Before borders:
Block size: 6-1/4"
Normal scale, five steps

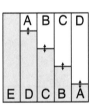

Make at least 112 blocks, identical or in several colors. Laura used 116 blocks and three color schemes. Make a mock-up block (see pages 12 and 18) for each color scheme.

	A	B	C	D
E	D	C	B	A

Fabric (if all blocks are same):

Dark fabrics	Light fabrics*
A = 1/3 yard	1/3 yard
B = 1/2 yard	1/2 yard
C = 3/4 yard	3/4 yard
D = 1 yard	1 yard
E = 1-1/8 yard	

Large background squares: 1 yard
Lining: 4 yards
*If all light fabrics are the same, use 2-1/3 yards.

1. Cut 45 strips:

Dark fabrics	Light fabrics
A = Five strips 2" x 44"	Five strips 2" x 44"
B = Five strips 3-1/4" x 44"	Five strips 3-1/4" x 44"
C = Five strips 4-1/2" x 44"	Five strips 4-1/2" x 44"
D = Five strips 5-3/4" x 44"	Five strips 5-3/4" x 44"
E = Five strips 7-1/4" x 44"	

2. Sew strips in pairs. Match mock-up blocks. Press seams toward the darker fabrics.

3. Prepare to cut sections. Pair off pieced strips like this, with right sides together:

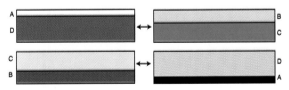

(Project 8 continued on page 70)

Scrap Quilts

Most Woodpile Quilts Look Scrappy

Most quilts in this book can be made with scraps instead of fat quarters or yardage. Often a piece smaller than 2" x 20" is all you need of a color. The general look is often scrappy, but you have the advantages of simplified cutting and organization and predictable block arrangement.

True Scrap Quilts

Now I'll also show you how to make true scrap quilts like the ones on this page, with fabrics mixed up so no two blocks are alike. The look is quite different, and so is the way you construct the blocks, as I explain on pages 75 and 76. You can use the scrap approach for almost any project in the book. It's more time-consuming, but scrap quilts are economical and sentimental and they show proper respect for the leftovers from other projects.

I made blocks for these 16-block projects at the same time so I could mix up sections for more variety. Do you notice a difference among these blocks? Can you spot those which have the light colors dominant? The Design-Your-Own charts on pages 61 to 64 include calculations for the light-dominant blocks.

Please read pages 75 and 76 before making scrap quilts.

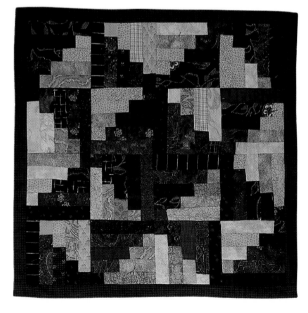

Sizzling 32 Quilts

Project 9 • Log Cabin Look-alike

This is one of the original Woodpile quilts which started it all, offered as an alternative to Log Cabin Quilts in my book, *Scrap Quilts Using Fast Patch* (1991).

Quilt size: About 64" x 82"
Block size: 9" square
Size: Large, six steps
Make 48 blocks, all with randomly mixed fabrics.

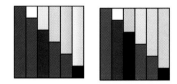

(No mock-up blocks are needed.)

Fabric

Dark fabrics:
   10 fat quarters*
   10 to 20 long scraps, at least 2" wide
   1/2 yard for inner border
   1 yard for outer border
Light fabrics:
   10 fat quarters*
Lining: 4 yards
*You can use scraps instead of fat quarters for all parts of the blocks.

1. Cut strips
a. Stack five Dark fat quarters evenly and cut through all layers, making five of each size:
   A = 2-1/4" x 21"
   C = 5-1/4" x 21"
   E = 8-1/4" x 21"
b. Stack five more Dark fat quarters and cut five of each size:
   D = 3-3/4" x 21"
   B = 6-3/4" x 21"
c. Trim the long Dark scraps to 2" x 10" (F strips). You will eventually need 48 of these. Cut the rest of them in Step 5 when you see which colors you need more of. You can use leftovers from the above steps if you wish.

d. Stack five Light fat quarters and cut these strips (five of each size):
   A = 2-1/4" x 21"
   C = 5-1/4" x 21"
   E = 8-1/4" x 21"
e. Stack five more Light fat quarters and cut these strips (five of each size):
   B = 3-3/4" x 21"
   D = 6-3/4" x 21"
Note: Set aside remnants promptly so they don't get mixed up with your strips!

(Project 9 continued on page 77)

Project 10 • Kelly's Sweetheart Quilt

Fifteen large hearts float on a light background in this delicate twin quilt. About half the blocks are Woodpile (pieced with an alternative method described on page 80). The other blocks are pieced with solid strips. Directions call for fat quarters (18" x 22") but you can use scraps if you wish. Betsy Hallock Heath, of Cheshire, Massachusetts, made this pretty quilt for her daughter Kelly, who was six when this picture was taken.

Quilt size: About 53" x 86"
Block size: 3-3/4" square
Size: Normal, three steps
Make 252 blocks:

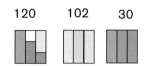

120   102   30

Arrange blocks into 15 hearts like this:

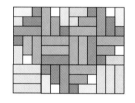

Sets of four light blocks fill extra space.

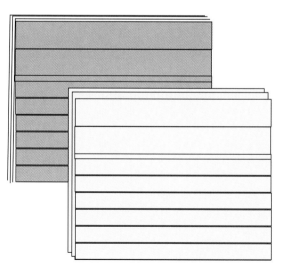

Fabric

Pink fabrics:
> Seven fat quarters, all different if possible
> 4" to 5" borders: 1 yard (Photo shows two 2-1/2" to 3" borders; use 1/2 yard for each.)

Light fabrics: 11 fat quarters (can repeat fabrics or use equivalent yardage)
> 2" inner border: 3/8 yard of any fabric already used
> Outer borders: 1/2 yard to 1 yard

Lining: About 4 yards, depending on border width

1. Cut 22"* strips.
Total 1-3/4" x 22" strips: 52 Pink, 82 Light
Total 3" x 22" strips: 10 Pink and 10 Light
Cutting suggestions:
a. Choose the two widest Pink fat quarters (a full 18" wide). Cut each into 10 strips 1-3/4" x 22".
b. Stack the other five Pink fat quarters and cut two stacks 3" x 22" and six stacks 1-3/4" x 22" (shown in art).
c. Cut two more 1-3/4" x 22" Pink strips from border fabric.
d. Stack six White/Light fat quarters and cut nine or 10 stacks of strips 1-3/4" x 22"

e. Stack the other five Light fat quarters. Cut two stacks of strips 3" x 22", then six more stacks of A strips 1-3/4" x 22" (shown in art).

*If any fat quarters are not quite 22" long, it will be okay. You can simply cut a few individual pieces in Step 5 to make up shortages.

(Project 10 continued on page 80)

Stitch and Flip Triangles

Hot Idea: Add Triangles

The most popular way to embellish Woodpile blocks is to add triangles with the easy "Stitch and Flip" method. I'll show two ways to apply triangles.

1. Add triangles after completing the blocks.
This is the easiest. Make any size blocks, trim and square them up, then add triangles to the dark corner. Here's one example, at left, which Christine Kamon of West Chester, Pennsylvania, made as a variation of Project 11 on page 36.

2. Add triangles before blocks are assembled.
This is much more exacting, but the design effect is more exciting because the triangles form pinwheels. The examples below are larger versions of Project 13 on page 39.

Right: This quilt is by Susan Grzeskowiak, owner of the Quilted Cactus shop in Yucca Valley, California.

Left: This quilt is by Christine Williams, also of Yucca Valley, California.

Project 11 • Fancy Paths

This easy wall hanging made by Pam Mennis of Norwich, New York, has blocks in two colors. Green strips form a path up and down the quilt while the purple print forms a path across. Triangles added to the dark corners make an interesting interchange at the intersections.

Quilt size: 33" square
Block size: 4-1/2"
Large scale, three steps

Make 36 blocks, 18 of each

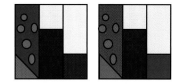

Blocks are arranged into clusters like this:

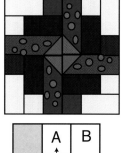

Make two mock-up blocks. Copy the three-step master on page 87 and add triangles, or just sketch your own. Suggestions: Use the same Dark B fabric in both blocks. For Dark A use a deeper shade of the fabric used for Dark C in the opposite block.

Fabric

Light A (blocks plus border): 1/3 yard
Single strips of three other lights (See Step 1)
Dark B (both types of blocks plus border): 5/8 yard
Single strips of four other darks (See Step 1)
Lining: 1 yard
Batting and binding as needed

1. Cut 14 strips.
a. Cut eight strips, one of each size for each color scheme.

Light fabrics	Dark fabrics
A = 2" x 38"	2" x 38"
B = 3-1/2" x 38"	3-1/2" x 38" (same color in both)

b. Cut six strips for tandem piecing and triangles, three from each C color 2" x 44".
2. Sew A and B strips together. Press toward the darks.
3. Lay out A and B panels for cutting cross-sections. Pair off as shown, with right sides together.

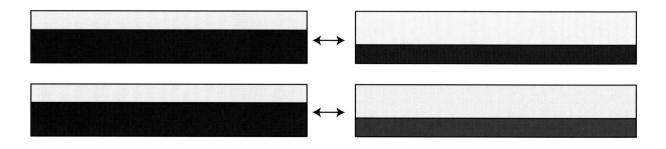

(Project 11 continued on page 82)

Making Pinwheels with Stitch and Flip Triangles

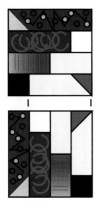

The next three projects need more advanced sewing skills because you have eight seams to line up. Use Normal and Large scale only; smaller sizes are always harder. Triangles are added before the blocks are assembled, so there's a new rule: Do not trim the top and bottom of the block. Trimming would obviously spoil the triangles. Sew accurately so ends are even and everything lines up. It's even more important to make a test block. New strip widths (with no 1/4" trimming allowance) and mock-up blocks are on pages 87 and 88.

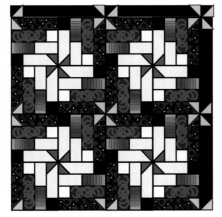

Pinwheels on the Edges?

Triangles are usually added to two corners of each block to make Pinwheels in both the dark and the light areas. It's much easier to omit the triangles around the edges of the quilt, in which case some blocks would have just one triangle. If you choose to keep triangles along the edge, make triangles in the first border also to complete the Pinwheels. Directions will be given with each project.

How to Add Triangles to Make Pinwheels

1. Cut squares the width of the cross-sections (usually 2").

2. Line up squares with light strips. Sew corner to corner at this angle.

3. Sew squares to dark strips at the same angle.

4. Trim seams to 1/4" and press to make triangles. (Press seams toward the center to avoid bulk later.)

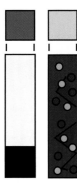

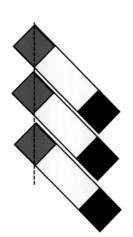

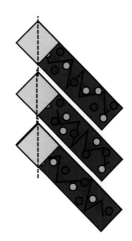

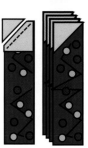

Project 12 • Toasted Triangles

Joanne Bodine of Elk Grove, California, started this beautiful quilt at a Fast Patch Retreat and finished it on her own. In addition to having triangles break into the first border, she added a Flying Geese border (sorry, no directions are given). Feel free to surround any project in this book with an imaginative pieced or appliquéd border.

Quilt size: About 43" x 52" with only inner borders (63" x 72" as shown)
Block size: 4-1/2"
Large scale, three steps
Make 80 blocks, all identical

You'll also need 18 border units like this and four sets of corner triangles.

Make a mock-up block (see pages 12 and 18).

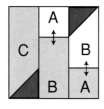

Fabric

Dark fabrics	Light fabrics
A = 1/4 yard	1/4 yard
B = 1 yard (incl. border)	3/8 yard
C = 1 yard (incl. border)	

Red (for 200 triangles): 2/3 yard
Lining: About 1-1/2 to 3 yards depending on borders.

1. Cut 20 strips, 44"* long:

Dark fabrics	Light fabrics
A = Four strips 2" x 44"	Four strips 2" x 44"
B = Four strips 3-1/2" x 44"	Four strips 3-1/2" x 44"
C = Four strips 5" x 44"	

2. Sew strips together like this:

*For this project, strips can be as short as 41". Prefer fat quarters? Cut eight strips at least 21" long of each.

3. Cut 2" cross-sections. Stack all of the same colors together (four layers) right sides up. Cut each stack into 20 cross-sections. You need a total of 80 of each color.

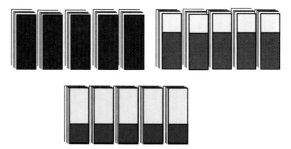

(Project 12 continued on page 83)

Project 13 • Housewarming

Here is the most common size of block to use when making Stitch and Flip Pinwheels. Triangles break into the border this time. Lois Stoltenberg, now of Chehalis, Washington, started this pretty little quilt in a class at the Something to Crow About quilt shop in Springfield, Oregon.

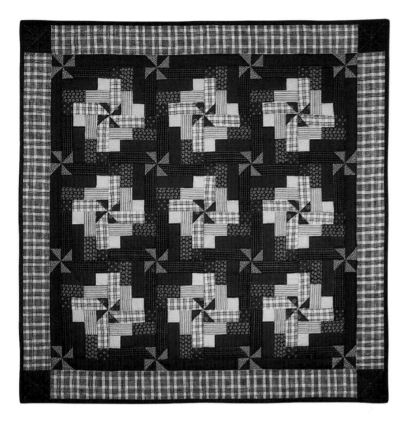

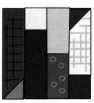

Quilt size: About 43" square
Block size: 6" square
Large scale, four steps
Total blocks: 36, identical

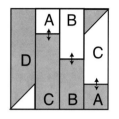

Make a mock-up block to determine colors. Draw your own or use the master on page 88.

Fabric

Dark fabrics	Light fabrics
A = 1/8 yard	1/8 yard
B = 1/4 yard	1/4 yard
C = 1/3 yard	3/4 yard (incl. border)
D = 1/2 yard	

Light or bright accent: 1/4 yard
Dark accent: 1/4 yard
Pieced border: 1/4 yard
Lining: 1-1/4 yard

1. Cut 14 strips. Cut two strips of each size:

Dark fabrics	Light fabrics
A = 2" x 38"	2" x 38"
B = 3-1/2" x 38"	3-1/2" x 38"
C = 5" x 38"	5" x 38"
D = 6-1/2" x 38"	

2. Sew together as shown. Press toward the dark.
3. Lay out panels for cutting sections.
a. These panels are simply stacked with identical panels, everything right side up.

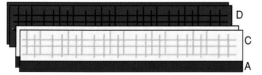

b. Panels below are aligned in pairs, right sides together for cutting.

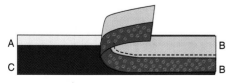

4. Cut 2" cross-sections. You will need 36 of each type. Leave sections stacked like this for sewing.

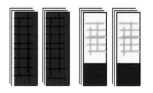

(Project 13 continued on page 84)

Project 14 • Glowing Pinwheels

This quilt, started at a Fast Patch retreat by Betty Hawkins of Gig Harbor, Washington, and machine quilted by Ione Whitney of Port Orchard, Washington, won a blue ribbon at the 1998 West Sound Quilters' show.

Quilt size: About 60" x 72" (add borders for a quilt about 70" x 82")
Block size: 6"
Large scale, four steps

Make 120 blocks, 40 of each color scheme, some with one triangle and some with two.

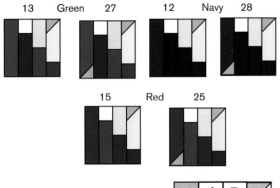

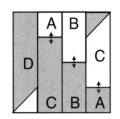

Make three mock-up blocks (see pages 12 and 18).

One key to success with this project is finding just the right fabrics for the transition between green and red. I call those colors "Navy," but Dark C is actually black with a subdued purple print. Dark D is a black print with subtle hints of green and red, which are very important.

Fabric

A = 1/4 yard cuts of six fabrics: Green, Navy, Red and three Lights*
B = 1/4 yard cuts of six fabrics: Green, Navy, Red and three Lights*
C = 1/3 yard cuts of six fabrics: Green, Navy, Red and three Lights*
D = 1/2 yard cuts of three fabrics: Green, Navy, Red
Gold: 5/8 yard
Lining: 3-2/3 yards (4 yards if borders are added)

*To simplify fabric selection, you can use the same Lights in all blocks. In that case you will need:
Light
A = 3/8 yard
B = 2/3 yard
C = 1 yard

(Project 14 continued on page 85)

More Information

When it comes to creative arts, I don't usually follow someone else's directions exactly, and you don't need to either. Throughout the book you'll find two features which will help you exercise your own creativity: Anita's Sketchbook and Design-Your-Own pages.

<u>*Anita's Sketchbook*</u>

Small Quilts

These pages give block layouts. Even if you don't care to design a quilt from scratch, you can use them to expand a quilt or make a smaller version, or to save a struggling quilt. Combining different fabrics is like mixing chemicals—unexpected things might happen. If you don't like the effect you are getting, switch to another layout, or just another way to arrange colors. Here is the same layout with colors distributed three different ways:

 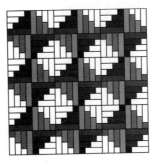 

I found literally hundreds of ways to combine blocks. It would have intimidated the faint of heart if I had included all of them (and the book would have cost twice as much). Instead I usually give 16-block designs, then give you lots of ways to expand them into large quilts on your own.

All the diagrams are the same scale, so really serious designers can photocopy these pages, cut out the windows, laminate the sheets, and use them as overlays to try hundreds of combinations:

Regular blocks, with H/V centers: 45
Regular blocks, with V/H centers: 49
Regular + Reverse blocks, with H/V centers: 124
Regular + Reverse blocks, with V/H centers: 128

Design-Your-Own Pages

Use these charts to make up your own project. The basic directions are pretty standard. Just make some blocks with that same method, using the chart on page to find the lengths and doing some simple math. Look through the book for an arrangement you like. Spread out the blocks and play with them.

Boldly Go Where No One Has Gone Before

Feel free to add creative touches of your own. See Project 12 (page 38) for creative borders. Look at the design on the back cover. Check out Celeste's quilt on page 112. There may be a follow-up Woodpile book with ideas that I didn't have room to develop, or ideas I think up after we go to press—or ideas that never occurred to me but were suggested by you, who bring your own quiltmaking experience and your own imagination. Stay in touch. Check the Internet for my web page (see page 157).

Overall Arrangements for Almost Any Quilt

Before getting to 16-block arrangements, let's check out some overall arrangements.

Here's my favorite arrangement. Use it for any number of blocks:

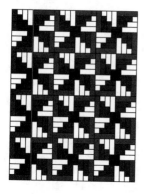

Here's the same design with colors distributed creatively:

Another good arrangement. Have an even number of blocks this direction:

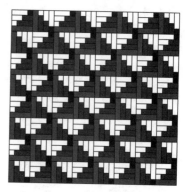

Tip: Use an L-frame to visualize smaller quilts.

If a layout shows 64 blocks, but you want to make a smaller quilt, block off part of the diagram, using this artist's trick.

1. Cut two L shapes. (I show how to use a business card; paper is okay.)

2. Overlap the frames to show only the number of blocks you want to make.

Cut

At least 2"

Draw a rectangle about 1"x2". Cut it like this. Discard the center.

At least 1-1/2"

Cut

For example:

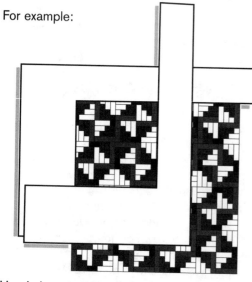

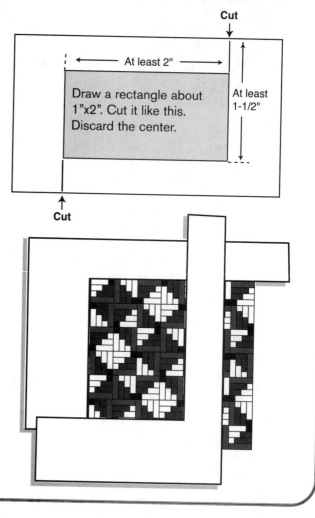

Here's how to take a layout from page 43 and focus on parts of it with the L-Frames.

Anita's Sketchbook

More Overall Patterns

These quilts need an even number of blocks in both directions. (Each pair uses the same arrangement—where the edges are changes the effect!)

 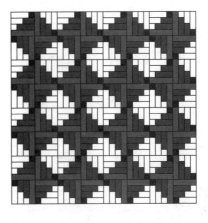

16-block Arrangements with Circle Centers (H/V)

There are dozens of ways you can arrange 16 blocks. The shades of gray give some suggestions for color distribution, but you usually have other creative options. Reading from left to right, blocks have horizontal, then vertical seams; hence the H/V designation.

Here are eight designs with dark circles in the center.

On this side are the same arrangements, with light circles in the center.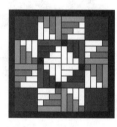

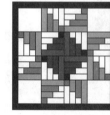

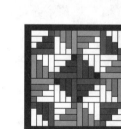
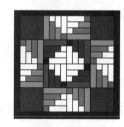

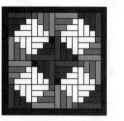
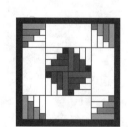

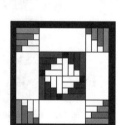

Some of these 16-block arrangements aren't that great as finished designs, but they are nice as centers for larger quilts, as you'll see in following pages.

Expand Quilts on Page 44 with a Border of Blocks

Make a 36-block quilt by placing 20 blocks around any of the designs on page 44. (Some of the blocks can be plain, of course, so you might need only 12 or 16 pieced blocks.)

Continue to Expand the Quilt with More Borders

A layout from page 44 (colors adapted):

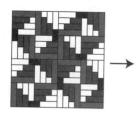

Plus a border from page 45:

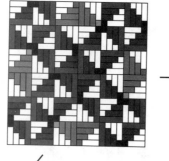

Plus another border, making 64 blocks:

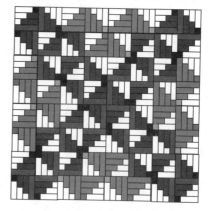

You don't need to add to all sides equally. Here blocks were added to the top and bottom only.

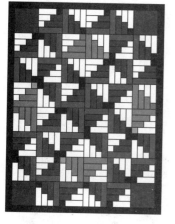

And another border, making 100 blocks:

Another good border to expand 36 to 64 blocks.

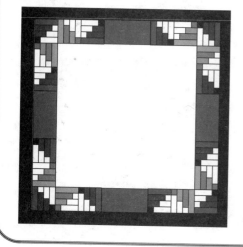

Other pages to check out:

• Pages 48 to 50 have similar ideas for blocks that start with Pinwheel centers.
• Pages 71 to 74 have large quilts, some built up this way.

In the second half of the book, pages 125 and 129 have similar ideas for projects with Reverse blocks added.

The possibilities are endless—I'd like to write another book just on borders. Until then, experiment on your own.

16-block Designs Combined to Make
64-block Designs

Here's how some of the 16-block arrangements on page 44 look when they are combined:

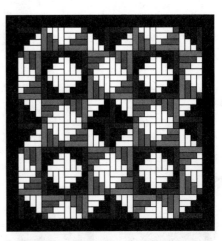

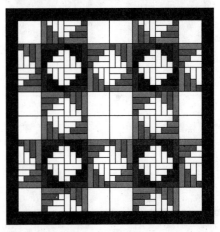

16-block Arrangements with Pinwheel Centers (V/H)

For a really dynamic look, make the center a Pinwheel. The design will revolve clockwise or counter-clockwise, depending on colors and shapes in the outer part of the design. There are two ways to make Pinwheels.

1. Make Pinwheels this way if blocks are all the same colors and you like the revolving "blades."

2. If you have at least two different color schemes (with contrast in the small squares), try it this way.

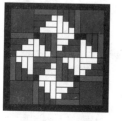
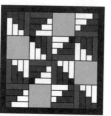

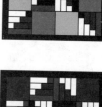

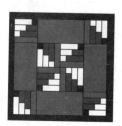

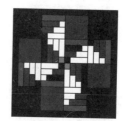
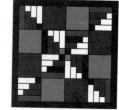

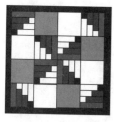
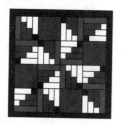
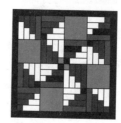

Double Your Designs

I found way too many ideas to fit on this page, but these sketches show the main effects you can get. You can automatically double the number of designs by making the Pinwheel in the middle revolve the opposite way. Double your options again by reversing the darks and lights. The effect is often very different!

Expand Pinwheel Quilts with a Border of Blocks

Use these borders to expand the arrangements on page 48. They all have plain blocks, usually in the corners.

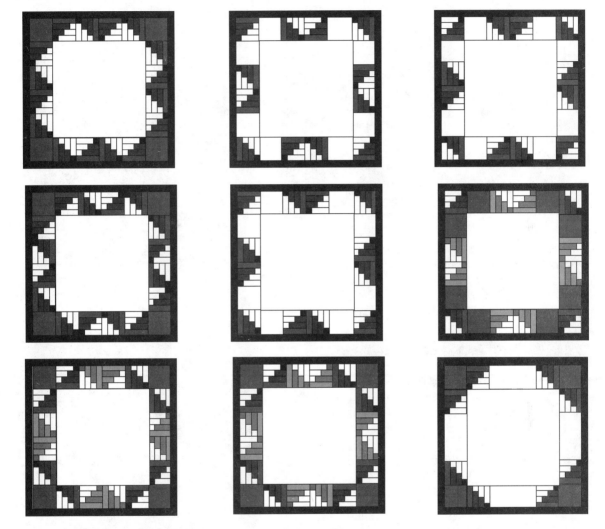

A serious designer can photocopy this page, cut out the windows and laminate the sheet. View different 16-block designs through the windows. Here are some of my favorite combinations:

  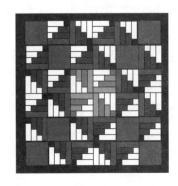

Expand Pinwheel Arrangements with Additional Borders

Start with a 16-block design from page 48 and build it up with one layer of borders after another.

16-block design
from page 48:

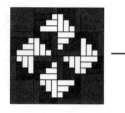

A border design from page 49:

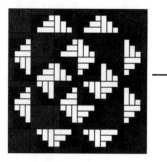

Another border:

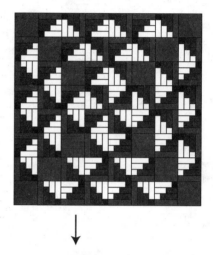

When building up a design, use a bold center and have it remain the most important part of the design. Don't let the border overpower the center.

Circle and Pinwheel Balance Sheet

The more you experiment with Circle and Pinwheel motifs, the more you'll see the advantages of each.

Final border (unless you want to keep going):

Want to build up from the center?

You'll probably be more satisfied when you start with a circle motif (see page 44). Choices for borders around Pinwheel designs are more limited.

Want to repeat 16-block designs to make 64 or more blocks?

Pinwheel designs are more exciting, as you'll see on the next page.

Want to develop an original design which doesn't follow either pattern?

You'll probably use Pinwheels; see pages 52 to 54, 60, and 71 to 74.

Want to mix and match designs and borders from pages 44 to 47 with those on pages 48 to 51?

Sorry, you can't do that, because the horizontal and vertical seams don't match. (However, as soon as you tell an innovative quilt artist she "can't do that," she'll find a way to do it. She'll put a solid border in between Woodpile borders, or put some plain blocks in critical spots, or just break the horizontal, vertical rule.)

16-block Pinwheel Designs Combined to Make 64-block Designs

Here's how some of the 16-block arrangements on page 48 would look combined to make 64 blocks. There are many other good possibilities. (Some of these have had colors modified or other slight changes; that's something you should expect to do also. See Project 2 on pages 23 and 56 for an example.)

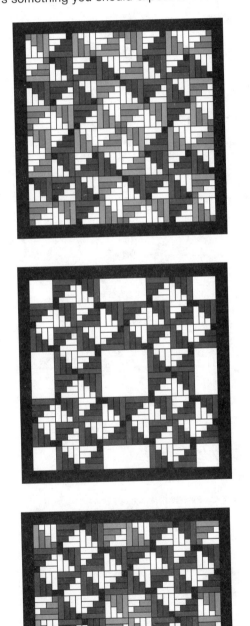
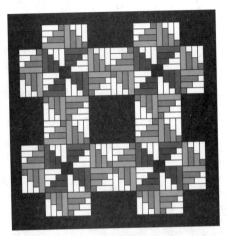
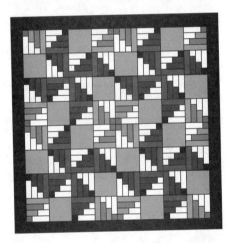
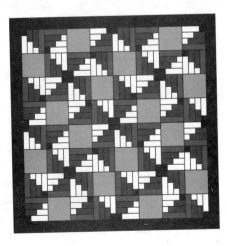

Anita's Sketchbook

More Ideas for Pinwheel Designs

This is a variation of Rain Dance,
Project 3, on page 24.

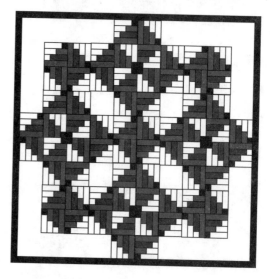

Pinwheels On Point

If using 52 blocks, Normal size, this would be about 70" square before borders. The colors could create an interesting effect here (if D strips were a bright color, for example).

This would be a fairly quick way to make a large quilt; 120 blocks 5" square would make a quilt about 72" x 86" before borders. There would be few seams to line up. Use white plus basically one color.

More Pinwheel Ideas

Here are two more ideas for Pinwheels. Also look at pages 71 to 74 for my sketchbook of ideas for designing large quilts; several quilts there feature Pinwheels.

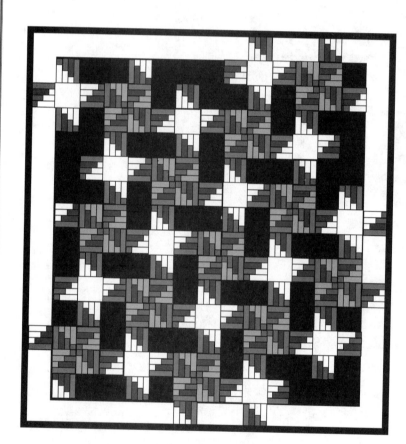

(Project 1, Super 16, continued from page 22)

9. Arrange the blocks to make a design. Turn alternate blocks on their sides so few seams need to line up. The smallest square usually must line up with neighboring blocks. (If any are not exactly 1-1/2" square, try to use them around the outer edge.)

Here's how to arrange the blocks as shown on page 22:

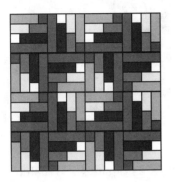

Before sewing the blocks together, try other arrangements on pages 32, 44, and 48. Also consider making a larger quilt with the optional steps on the right.

10. Add borders. To match Susan's quilt:

a. Cut a 1" border from a bright accent fabric. Two 44" strips should make all borders if you are careful. (Susan actually made a three-dimensional border by sewing a folded strip into the seam.)

b. Cut three 2" x 44" strips from any dark fabric. Cut one in two for top and bottom. Cut sides from the other two strips. Sew them in place.

c. Add four 3-1/2" wide strips for the outer borders.

11. Quilt and bind with your favorite method. Susan machine quilted diagonally both directions making an "X" through each block.

Ways to expand Project 1

Repeat Steps 1 to 8 with another color scheme. You might choose to use 36" strips to make 20 blocks this time (if you make only 16, plan to add four plain blocks). Keep a contrast among the four colors in the Dark A and D positions. The expanded quilt size will be about 30" square before borders and about 40" after final borders.

Mix up colors

Use eight blocks with the new color scheme in the inner quilt, and use eight of the original blocks in the outer part.

Find a design you like

If you used the arrangement on the left—or another one with a circle in the center—add a border from page 45. If you used a Pinwheel center, use a border from page 49. Add plain blocks (5-1/2" square) as needed.

Feel free to use a design which isn't shown. I didn't have room to show all the possibilities; you might find one that suits you better.

Make a total of 48 blocks to match Muriel Erlandson's quilt on page 17.

(Project 2, Marcella's Quilt, continued from page 23)

7. Make 48 blocks.
a. Continue to spot-check to make sure blocks are 5-1/2" wide.
b. Press toward the darker area.
c. Trim blocks as on page 15, making sure the small dark A pieces are 1-1/2" square.

8. Make 12 or 16 blocks from the second color scheme. Follow Steps 1 to 7. The example on page 23 (and below) uses only 12 of these blocks, but it's nice to have all 16 to experiment with.

9. Arrange blocks.
a. Arrange 16 blocks into a design. Use the one below, or try any of the designs on page 44 or 48.
b. Repeat the design four times. See pages 47 and 51.
c. Make creative modifications to improve the arrangement.

10. When you are satisfied, sew the blocks together.

Sometimes "less is more." This design uses only 48 blocks. See page 21 for this arrangement in color. Use any leftover blocks to start another project.

11. Add borders as desired. To match the sample, cut borders like this:
a. Cut four strips 1-3/4" wide for the inner borders.
b. Cut four strips 3" to 5" wide for the outer borders.
c. Cut four squares that same width for the corners.

12. Quilt and bind with your favorite method.

Rotated 180 degrees.

Rotated

Rotated

Plain blocks used in corners

Rotated

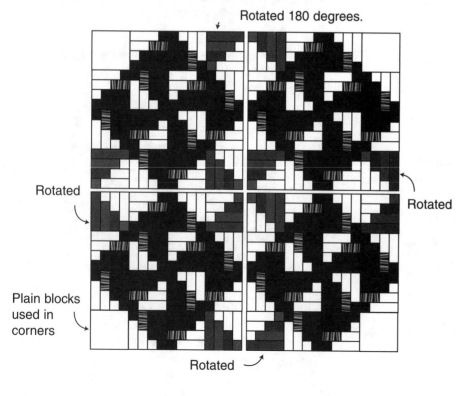

(Project 3, Rain Dance, continued from page 24)

5. Sew pairs together. Use a scant 1/4" seam. Keep the largest light pieces on top.

6. Assemble eight blocks.

a. Make a test block. Sew pairs together, press, and measure the block. It should be 5-1/2" wide.

b. Make eight blocks, using the exact seam width needed.

c. Trim ends, starting with the small dark square (arrow). Make sure it is exactly 1-1/2" square. See page 15.

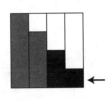

7. Make 16 more blocks. Repeat steps 2 to 6 to make eight blocks from each of the other sets of strips.

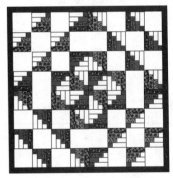

8. Cut background pieces.

a. Cut eight pieces 5-1/2" x 11" (10-1/2" if you don't add striped inserts). Using directional fabric? Cut half the double blocks the other direction.

b. Cut eight pieces 5-1/2" square.

9. Add striped inserts (optional).

a. Cut strips of striped fabric, 3/4" to 1" wide:
Two 5-1/2"
Two 10-1/2"
One 21-1/2"

b. Sew between blocks like this:

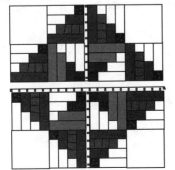

10. Assemble the quilt top.

a. Join sections of the quilt in the order shown. If you aren't using striped inserts, you might want to change the color arrangement to give contrast where four small squares come together.

b. Add borders. To match the sample on page 24, add:

• 1" striped borders
• Borders about 2-1/4" wide
• 1" striped borders
• Outer borders up to 5". Cut five 44" strips.

11. Quilt and bind with your favorite methods.

36 blocks

28 blocks

Note: If you want to make a few more blocks, here are a couple of ways to vary this project (also see pages 48 to 54):

(Project 4, Christmas Table Runner, continued from page 25)

7. Complete 12 blocks. Continue to line up red seams and maintain the exact seam width for 5-1/2" blocks.

8. Make 12 blocks with gold lamé and black squares.

9. Sew blocks together (see page 25).

a. Sew identical blocks together in pairs.

b. Sew 12 blocks together, alternating colors, as shown in the diagram.

c. Make an identical set of 12 blocks (colors in the exact same position). Reverse it.

d. Combine the two rows of blocks. The red squares will spiral across the design, with black squares spiraling the opposite way.

10. Add triangles to the ends. Cut an 8" square of green fabric apart diagonally. Add one triangle to each end.

11. Add borders. You need to miter 45° corners plus the ends. Here's one way to do it:

a. Cut four 2-1/2" x 44" strips from your border/lining fabric.

b. Piece together two long pieces. Sew them to each side, centered, stopping 1/4" from the corner.

c. Sew an angled seam (tuck) at each corner. Baste first, check, then sew at the correct angle.

d. Miter the ends as usual.

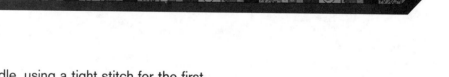

12. Make the lining.

a. Cut two 15" x 40" lengths.

b. Sew them together in the middle, using a tight stitch for the first 2" (white dot), basting most of the seam, then sewing a tight stitch again for the last couple of inches.

c. Cut the lining to match the front.

d. With right sides together, stitch the front and back together 1/2" from all edges.

13. Finish the project.

a. Pick out the basting in the lining.

b. Turn the project right side out, press the edges neatly, and hand stitch to close the opening.

c. Do any quilting desired, including stitching around the edge of the border.

d. Stitch gold metallic trim to the edge of the border by machine or by hand.

Anita's Sketchbook

Table Runners with 24 Blocks

These examples show two different color schemes, 12 blocks of each type. They could all be the same color scheme. See the photo on page 18.

 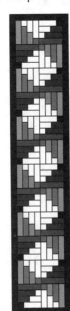 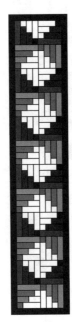 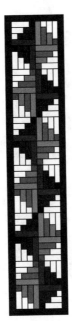 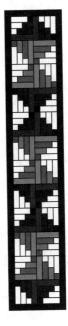 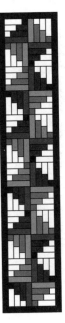

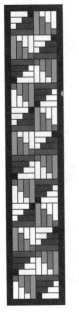 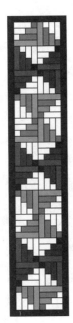  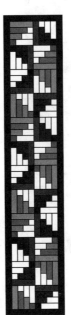

I show only plain blocks. Could you substitute the blocks from Project 4 (page 25) with the contrasting squares down the middle? If you have started that project but not sewn the blocks together, try some of these arrangements and the ones on the next page. The chains of squares would certainly change the effect.

More Ideas for Table Runners

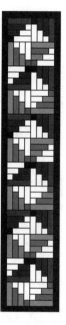
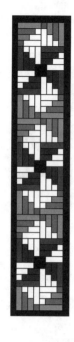
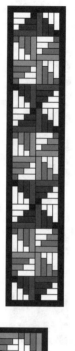
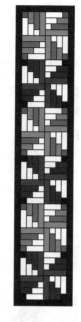
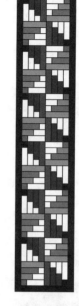
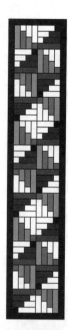

Of course, you should feel free to adapt these ideas to other lengths, or to any other projects that appeal to you.

Three Steps

(Note: I'll have many charts like this for planning your own projects. I have comments on this one to show how the charts work.

Standard (Dark dominant) Step height

Alternate (Light dominant)

Widths to make alternate version.

Block size (after seams)	2-1/4" (Mini)	3" (Small)	3-3/4" (Normal)	4-1/2" (Large)	
Step height	3/4"	1"	1-1/4"	1-1/2"	
Dark C	2-3/4"	3-1/2"	4-1/4"	5"	C **Light**
Light A	1-1/4"	1-1/2"	1-3/4"	2"	A **Dark**
Dark B	2"	2-1/2"	3"	3-1/2"	B **Light**
Light B	2"	2-1/2"	3"	3-1/2"	B **Dark**
Dark A	1-1/4"	1-1/2"	1-3/4"	2"	A **Light**
Cut sections this wide	1-1/4"	1-1/2"	1-3/4"	2"	

The chart above gives the width of the strips. (See page 65 for lengths.)

=
=
=

Bottom numbers tell how wide to cut the cross sections

Tip: To focus on the size and version you are making:
1. Photocopy the page.
2. Trim off everything you don't need to avoid confusion.
3. Mark the column you're using.
4. Write the total length needed (from the chart on page 65).
5. Tape the sheet to your cutting mat or keep it handy.
Here are two examples:

44"

29"

Design-Your-Own

Four Steps

Standard

Includes 1/4" allowance for trimming

Alternate

Block size (after seams)	3" (Mini)	4" (Small)	5" (Normal)	6" (Large)	
Step height	3/4"	1"	1-1/4"	1-1/2"	
Dark D	4"	5"	6"	7"	D **Light**
Light A	1-1/2"	1-3/4"	2"	2-1/4"	A **Dark**
Dark C	3"	3-3/4"	4-1/2"	5-1/4"	C **Light**
Light B	2-1/4"	2-3/4"	3-1/4"	3-3/4"	B **Dark**
Dark B	2-1/4"	2-3/4"	3-1/4"	3-3/4"	B **Light**
Light C	3"	3-3/4"	4-1/2"	5-1/4"	C **Dark**
Dark A	1-1/2"	1-3/4"	2"	2-1/4"	A **Light**
Cut sections this wide	1-1/4"	1-1/2"	1-3/4"	2"	

Design-Your-Own

Five Steps

Standard

Includes 1/4" allowance for trimming

Alternate

Block size (after seams)	3-3/4" Mini	5" Small	6-1/4" Normal	7-1/2" Large	
Step width	3/4"	1"	1-1/4"	1-1/2"	
Dark E	4-3/4"	6"	7-1/4"	8-1/2"	E **Light**
Light A	1-1/2"	1-3/4"	2"	2-1/4"	A **Dark**
Dark D	3-3/4"	4-3/4"	5-3/4"	6-3/4"	D **Light**
Light B	2-1/4"	2-3/4"	3-1/4"	3-3/4"	B **Dark**
Dark C	3"	3-3/4"	4-1/2"	5-1/4"	C **Light**
Light C	3"	3-3/4"	4-1/2"	5-1/4"	C **Dark**
Dark B	2-1/4"	2-3/4"	3-1/4"	3-3/4"	B **Light**
Light D	3-3/4"	4-3/4"	5-3/4"	6-3/4"	D **Dark**
Dark A	1-1/2"	1-3/4"	2"	2-1/4"	A **Light**
Cut sections this wide	1-1/4"	1-1/2"	1-3/4"	2"	

Design-Your-Own

Six Steps

Standard

Includes 1/4" allowance for trimming

Alternate

Block size (after seams)	4-1/2" Mini	6" Small	7-1/2" Normal	9" Large	
Step width	3/4"	1"	1-1/4"	1-1/2"	
Dark F	5-1/2"	7"	8-1/2"	10"	F **Light**
Light A	1-1/2"	1-3/4"	2"	2-1/4"	A **Dark**
Dark E	4-1/2"	5-3/4"	7"	8-1/4"	E **Light**
Light B	2-1/4"	2-3/4"	3-1/4"	3-3/4"	B **Dark**
Dark D	3-3/4"	4-3/4"	5-3/4"	6-3/4"	D **Light**
Light C	3"	3-3/4"	4-1/2"	5-1/4"	C **Dark**
Dark C	3"	3-3/4"	4-1/2"	5-1/4"	C **Light**
Light D	3-3/4"	4-3/4"	5-3/4"	6-3/4"	D **Dark**
Dark B	2-1/4"	2-3/4"	3-1/4"	3-3/4"	B **Light**
Light E	4-1/2"	5-3/4"	7"	8-1/4"	E **Dark**
Dark A	1-1/2"	1-3/4"	2"	2-1/4"	A **Light**
Cut sections this wide	1-1/4"	1-1/2"	1-3/4"	2"	

Design-Your-Own

Total Lengths of Strips Needed

Charts on pages 61 to 64 tell how wide to make the strips. The length depends on the scale and number of blocks. This chart will help.

Figures allow for error; you can usually use slightly shorter strips. If your fabric is 43" wide, for example, and the chart says 44" strips, go ahead and use 43, and cut cross-sections carefully. If you can't cut all of the sections you need, just cut individual pieces from scraps for the last block.

Number of blocks	Mini	Small	Normal	Large
8	11"	13"	15"	17"
10	14"	16"	18"	21"
12	16"	19"	22"	25"
14	19"	21"	26"	29"
16	22"	25"	29"	33"
18	24"	28"	33"	37"
20	27"	32"	37"	41"
22	30"	35"	40"	45"
24	32"	38"	44"	50"
26	35"	42"	47"	54"
28	38"	45"	51"	58"
30	40"	48"	55"	62"
32	43"	51"	58"	66"

How Many Blocks Should You Make?

Sets of eight blocks are nice. It's easy to cut strips from fat quarters and you can combine as many sets as you want. Each set can have a different color scheme.
- Two sets make a 16-block wall hanging.
- Three sets make 24 blocks for a table runner or wall hanging.
- Four sets, plus a few plain squares, make a 36-block quilt.
- Six sets (or five sets plus plain blocks) make a baby quilt.

- Eight sets (or seven sets plus plain blocks) make a 64-block quilt.

Other multiples of four are good too. I often use sets of 12, 16, 20, or 24 blocks because most quilts are symmetrical (one corner is repeated four times). It's satisfying to distribute colors in a balanced and predictable way.

And, of course, you can have all blocks the same color. The quickest way to make a quilt is to have all blocks identical. Just choose an arrangement and make the total blocks needed.

7. Sew blocks together in sets of four. Press.

8. Cut squares from background fabric.

a. Measure the blocks (they should be 6-1/2" square). Cut 12 squares that size.

b. Cut four 10-1/2" squares. Cut them in fourths and label them "edges."

c. Cut two 6" squares. Cut them in half and label them "corners."

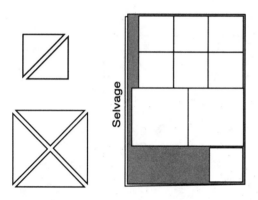

Here's one way to cut, through a double layer of fabric.

9. Partially assemble rows of blocks. Rotate blocks to mix colors up as you go.

a. Sew together eight patchwork blocks and eight plain blocks in sets of four like this: Have final seams in the blocks going in the direction of the arrows.

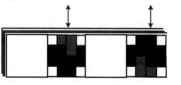

b. Sew four blocks to "side" triangles (final seams match the arrow). Make sure edges line up as shown.

c. Sew four blocks to side triangles, slanted the other way.

d. Sew two blocks to "corner" triangles, centered like this:

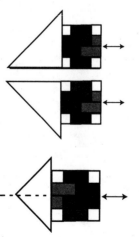

10. Piece together diagonal rows of blocks. Follow the diagram carefully:

11. Finish the quilt top

a. Sew rows together. You may have to widen the final seams of some blocks (arrows in Step 9A) so edges of blocks will line up evenly. Background triangles will overlap.

b. Press the quilt top.

c. Trim edges and square up the quilt. Leave a uniform area of background fabric around the edges.

d. For inner borders, cut four 2" x 44" strips (or wider) of brown fabric. Sew to sides first, then ends.

e. For outer borders, cut five strips 4" wide of green. Add top and bottom borders first this time because 44" strips should fit there without piecing. The side borders will need to be pieced.

12. Quilt and bind with your favorite methods. One way to quilt: Quilt with gentle curves which cross in the centers and at the corners of the blocks. Outline each set of blocks 1/4" from the edge, or quilt a simple design within the dark blocks.

Make Hearts Instead of Card Trick

When turned at an angle, this simple block makes a "Primitive Heart." To make them, pair off panels which both have the same color of fabric.

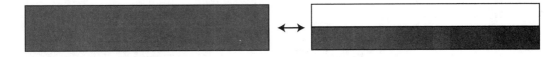

For horizontal rows, such as borders, join blocks and triangle background pieces like this:

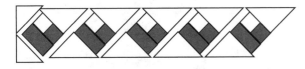

Cut 5-1/2" squares, one for every two hearts. Cut each into four triangles. Smaller triangles (3" squares cut in two) are used on the ends.

For vertical rows, sew blocks and triangles together like this:

(Project 6, Betsy's Pinwheels, continued from page 29)

5. Sew sections together. Keeping the larger light sections on top, sew with scant 1/4" seams, chaining like this:

6. Make a test block.

a. Combine sections.

b. Add a long (E) strip.

c. Press, measure, and trim the block as shown on page 15. It should be 6-3/4" square and the small dark A square must be 1-1/2".

7. Complete 24 blocks. Adjust seams to keep the blocks square.

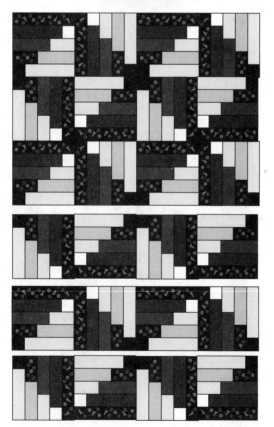

8. Make six rows of blocks.

a. Sew four blocks at a time into sets as shown. (All rows are the same; some will be rotated.)

b. Combine rows into a quilt top.

9. Add any borders you desire. Fabric allowances were for these widths:

a. Green borders 2-1/2" wide.

b. Light borders 2" wide.

c. Purple borders 4" wide.

10. Quilt and bind with your favorite methods. Some ideas for the quilting pattern:

a. Have it machine quilted with stippling or a pattern which doesn't follow the patchwork design.

b. Do echo quilting with light thread around the light design and a simple motif with dark thread in the dark area.

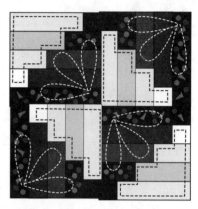

c. Do straight diagonal lines with dark thread (only if blocks are very accurate). Add a simple motif in the dark, then switch to light thread and do a simple motif in the light (below).

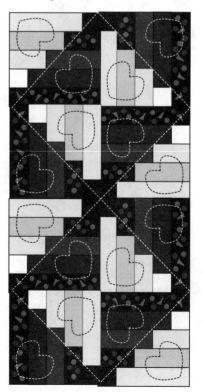

(Project 7, Seven Stars, continued from page 30)

6. Cut 25 plain blocks. Cut these the size of the Woodpile blocks (3-1/2" square):

Seven from Light

18 from Dark

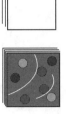

7. Assemble seven rows of blocks. Set four Woodpile blocks aside. They will be used in the borders. Sew the other blocks into seven rows like this:

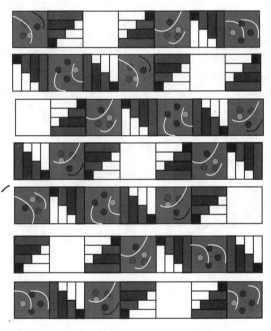

(Bottom three rows are identical to the top three rows, but are rotated.)

8. Sew the rows together.

9. Add borders.

a. If your blocks were exactly 3-1/2" square, cut sections for the pieced border this size:

 Two pieces 6-1/2" x 3-1/2"
 Two pieces 9-1/2" x 3-1/2"
 Two pieces 12-1/2" x 3-1/2"
 Two pieces 15-1/2" x 3-1/2"

(If using a directional fabric, study the artwork and cut these pieces carefully for a nice effect.)

b. Piece together border pieces and the four Woodpile blocks as shown and add to the quilt.

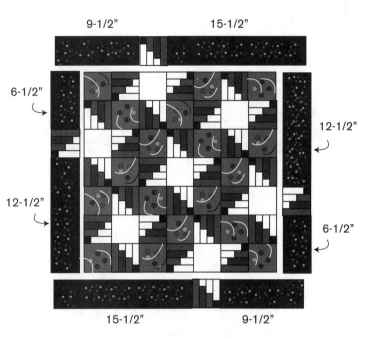

c. Add outer borders if desired. Cut borders 2" wide or any other width.

10. Layer, quilt, and bind as desired. Here is one idea for free-style machine quilting. Don't try to duplicate it exactly; just study it and do your own version of swirling curves in the dark areas and echo quilting in the light areas.

4. Cut 1-3/4" cross-sections.
a. Cut panels into cross-sections, 112 sets of each dark/light ratio. (Try to get 24 from each pair of strips). Stack neatly to sew without rearranging.
b. Cut the E panels (7-1/4" strips) into sections too. Just stack and cut all five layers at a time.

5. Make a test block.
a. Sew pairs together.
b. Join sewn pairs, plus an E strip.

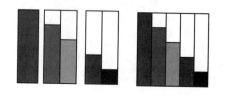

c. Press toward the darker side and measure to see if it's 6-3/4" wide.
d. Trim ends so the block is 6-3/4" square; the small square must be 1-1/2".
Adjust seam width, if necessary, for remaining blocks.
6. Make 112 blocks (116 for Laura's). Make sure blocks are 6-1/4" and small squares are 1-1/2".
7. Begin assembling blocks. See the box below. For an easy start (if blocks are identical):

Make six of these: Make seven of these:

8. Cut background squares. Use the same light used for blocks, or choose a new one. Lay out the blocks over different pieces of yardage and choose just the right one. Cut these sizes:

Eight pieces 6-3/4" square (four for Laura's version)
Six pieces 6-3/4" x 13"
Two pieces 13" square

Here's one way to cut them from 1 yard of fabric, folded over.

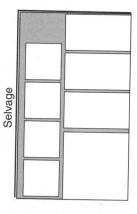

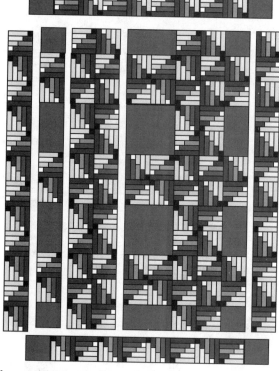

9. Assemble the quilt top.
10. Quilt and bind with your favorite methods.

Designing your quilt

The diagram above was my idea for the green quilt (page 31) Compare it with Laura's. Your quilt might not match either. Just play with your blocks and use each color in a predictable pattern. (If you made five color schemes, the positions won't match Laura's quilt since she used three.)

Laura made the neat heart pattern by reversing darks and lights around the edges. That created a design problem in the corners which she solved by breaking the alternating seams rule. It worked! You can get that same general effect by making four Reverse blocks. See page 90.

Large Quilts

On pages 44 and 48 are 16-block arrangements, 32 in all. With that many possibilities for 16 blocks, imagine the possibilities for a quilt with 36, 48, 64, 80, or 100 blocks. I can show only a few, so let's review how to design your own.

1. Start with an overall design and add a border of blocks. This is a good approach for a baby quilt or a simple, unpretentious bed quilt. Pick a design on page 41 or 42. Design a border, with inspiration from pages 45 and 49.

Tip: If you try to use borders on page 45 but the vertical/horizontal seams aren't compatible with the inner design, switch to borders from page 49, and vice versa.

2. Start with a 16-block design and add borders. You can build up the design with as many layers of borders as you wish. See pages 46 and 50 for a lot of ideas.

Notice that the outer border on the quilt at the right wouldn't fit if it were placed right next to the main part of the quilt. The seams are vertical when they should be horizontal. By adding a plain border in between, you can get around that restriction.

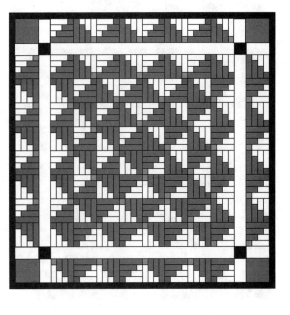

Anita's Sketchbook

3. Repeat a 16-block design several times, then add borders of blocks (see pages 47 and 51). Project 8 (page 31) is a good example of a 16-block design repeated six times and enclosed in a border. Creative changes can always be made.

4. Merge two different 16-block designs. Take a design from page 44 and one from page 48. Overlap them so they share some blocks (adjusting as necessary). Repeat to make as large a quilt as you want. And, of course, you can add one or two borders of blocks to these designs.

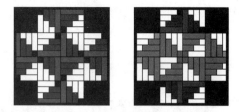

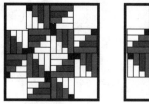

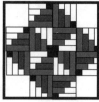

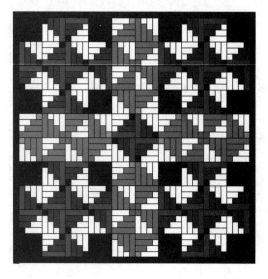

Anita's Sketchbook

5. Play with blocks and see what else you come
up with.

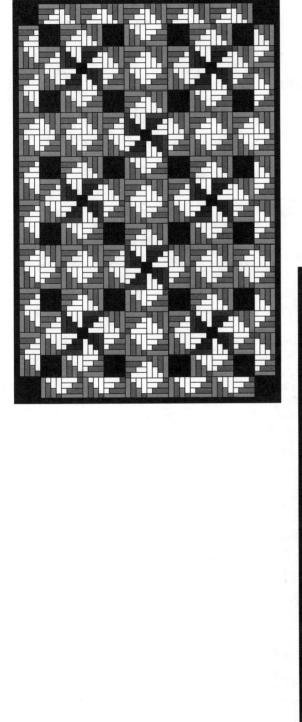

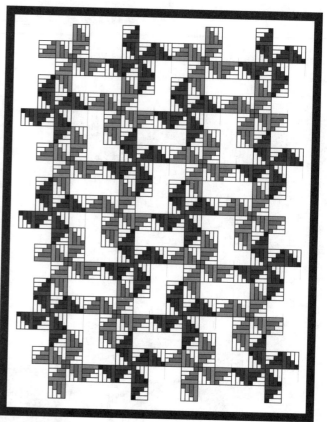

More Ideas

These ideas are just to get you started. You might start laying out one arrangement and discover something quite different.

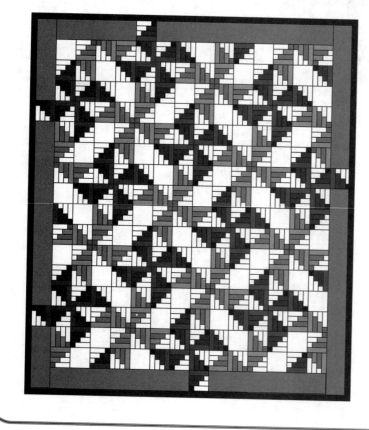

(Hot Idea continued from page 26)

Use a Different Approach for Scrap Quilts

Limited-fabric Quilts:

Design Considerations

Unless all blocks are identical, you'll have more creative decisions about where to use each color family.

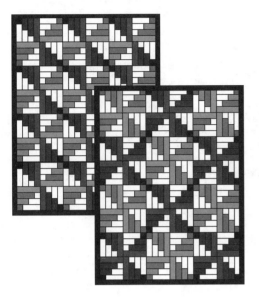

Mock-up blocks

Make one for each color scheme.

Choosing Fabrics

Choose a limited number of fabrics carefully. Keep colors and general fabric types compatible with each other.

Cutting and Sewing Strips

Cut all of your strips first for efficiency. Directions in specific projects spell out how many strips you need of each color. When you design your own (using the charts on pages 61 to 65) make your own list of strips needed.

Sewing strips together is quick because they are the same length and decisions have already been made

Scrap Quilts:

Design Considerations

Although there will be more variety among blocks, any block can usually be used anywhere.

Here is the same design shown on the left; however, you can choose to divide your scraps into distinct color schemes and use each in a specific area.

Mock-up Blocks

Not needed; no two blocks will be alike.

Choosing Fabrics

Choose dozens of fabrics, after deciding on dominant colors and your general fabric mood. If you buy coordinated packets of fat quarters or fat eighths, add similar fabrics from your own stash. You can use a few "ugly" colors if they don't distract from the rest of the quilt.

Cutting and Sewing Strips

"Estimate and add." Cut a variety of lengths to fit your scraps–but not as many as you think you'll need. As you complete some blocks, cut more strips of the colors you need and work them in.

If you have scraps of unequal length, trim them to match, or just butt the ends of the shorter strips up

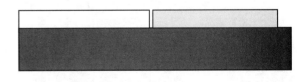

Limited-fabric Quilts:

Cutting and Stacking Sections

Line up two panels, right sides together, to cut cross-sections.

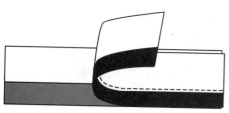

Stack sections in pairs ready to sew.

Assembling Blocks

Quick and easy—everything's organized and there are no decisions to make.

Scrap Quilts:

Cutting and Stacking Cross-sections

Stack panels with the same dark/light ratio, right side up, Light fabric on same edge.

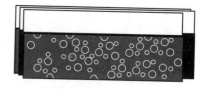

Offset seams (to avoid cutting through too much bulk), but keep seams parallel for accuracy.
Stack the same types of sections together, colors in random order, right sides up.

Assembling Blocks

You have to be well organized. See below.

Assembling Blocks for Scrap Quilts

Because each block is different, you're always choosing fabrics to combine. This is fun, but you can really make a mess by pawing through piles and looking for just the right section to use next. Arrange space by your sewing machine to spread out several piles of fabric and try one of these ideas:

1. Build up a couple of blocks at a time. Have two piles for each combination. As you look for just the right color, move sections from one pile to another, but keep them neat.

2. Or... Spread out several examples of one type of section. Build up dozens of blocks at the same time, adding the same type of section to each. Then put out the next sections and add them to each block.

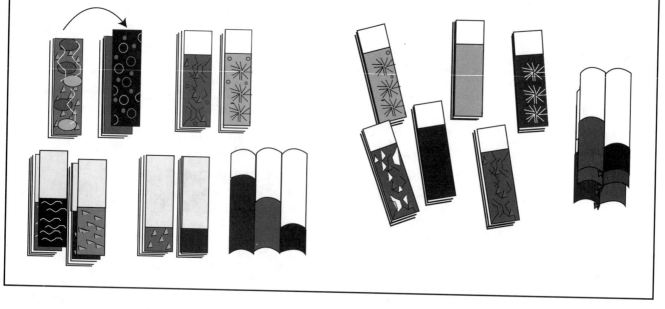

(Project 9, Log Cabin Look-alike, continued from page 33)

2. Make pairs. Set aside the 2" x 10" darks. Pair off the other strips and sew them together. Press toward the darks.

Tip: It's easy to goof and sew the wrong ones together. Pin them first and check before sewing each set to make sure the width of the two strips equals about 10".

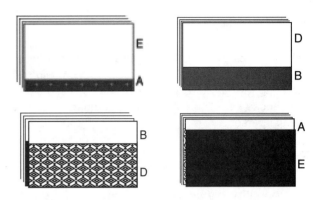

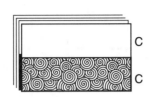

3. Cut cross-sections. With panels stacked as shown, cut all layers into 2" sections. You should get 10 from each (50 sections; you need 48).

4. Make a test block. Build up strips in this order, including a 2" x 10" (F) strip. Trim the block to 9-1/2" square. The small dark A must be exactly 1-3/4" square.

5. Make 48 blocks. (On the opposite page are hints about organizing your work so you can choose fabrics which look best together each time.) Spot-check to make sure blocks are 9-1/2" wide. Cut more 2" x 10" strips of new fabrics as needed for a nice color effect in each block.
6. Arrange blocks in rows of six. Notice that all rows have blocks in the same order but half of the rows are rotated.

Tip: Keep a good color contrast whenever the four small dark squares meet. If there are any blocks where those squares are not accurate, use them in the corners of the quilt where they don't have to line up with anything.

7. Sew rows together.

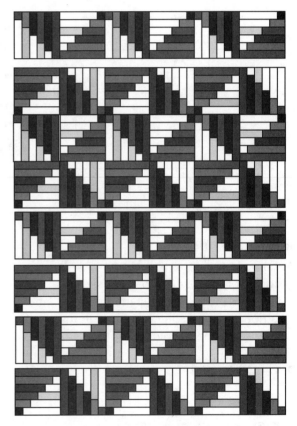

8. Add borders.
a. Cut seven or eight 2" x 44" strips from any fabric. Piece together as needed and sew to the quilt as inner borders.
b. Cut eight 4" x 44" strips for the outer borders.
9. Quilt and bind with your favorite method. Commercial machine quilting is a popular choice for scrap projects. (Also see page 68, Betsy's Pinwheels).

Friendship Quilt for a Group

The Log Cabin Look-alike, Project 9, makes a good group project. Better yet, do two quilts and mix up the parts. Decide on a color scheme so you don't get a hodgepodge of fabrics that don't look good together. Show the participants sample fabrics, or clip samples to the assignments. In addition to regular supplies, organizers should also furnish additional dark scraps and fabric pens for signing names.

Photocopy these assignments. For each twin quilt (48 blocks, about 64" x 82") make five copies. Cut them apart and give a slip to 10 people. (Or ask each person to make more than one set.) For a prettier quilt, have someone choose beautifully coordinated fat quarters and distribute them with the instructions, a light one and a dark one to each person.

- -

Friendship Quilt

1. Choose two fat quarters that look good together, one light and one dark. Use small or medium-size prints or plaids; no stripes or big, high-contrast patterns, please. General color or type

_____.

2. Cut both apart like this:

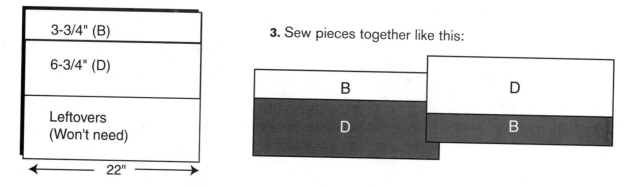

3. Sew pieces together like this:

Also bring several long dark scraps of compatible colors (big enough to cut 2" x 10" strips).

- -

Friendship Quilt

1. Choose two fat quarters that look good together, one light and one dark. Use small or medium-size prints or plaids; no stripes or big, high-contrast patterns, please. General color or type

_____.

2. Cut both apart like this:

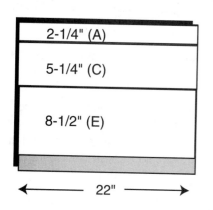

3. Sew pieces together like this:

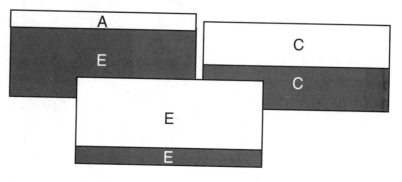

There are a lot of ways to arrange a group project. Individuals can each sew blocks from start to finish, or there can be people assigned to press and cut and square up blocks as other people sew. Only one sewing machine would be needed for each two or three people. Follow the instructions on page 77, starting with Step 3. Here are some special suggestions:

Autographs

After cutting cross-sections, choose some with large plain **light** areas (no busy print). Have each person sign her name or write a Bible verse, poem, or friendship message on the sections with indelible pens. Be sure to allow seam allowances. If any sections are messed up, just discard them. (You can sign finished blocks or even the quilted project, but there is some risk of messed up messages distracting from the quilt.)

3. Cut cross-sections. Distribute six piles of strips to each person who will be sewing, one stack of each type of cross-section, plus a stack of 2" x 10" **dark** strips.

4. Skip the test blocks? Instead of making test blocks, you might choose to just let people sew and have fun. Have a "corrections officer" to correct blocks with problems. Do monitor to make sure everyone understands that when they sew strips together the largest **light** sections go on top so blocks will automatically have the slant they need.

"Corrections Officer"

a. If blocks are too narrow, sew a 3/4" wide strip of striped fabric to the **dark** side. In addition to making the blocks wider, these strips add a fun accent that will unify blocks and make the project more interesting.

b. If some blocks are assembled wrong, and there are too many seams to pick out, set them aside. See "Lemonade" pages in the Appendix for a way to have fun with them.

c. If blocks are too wide or are tapered, widen seams as needed.

d. You still need the small **dark** (A) squares exactly 1-3/4" for virtually all projects. If it's too large, pick out the whole seam and reposition or replace that part of the block. If it's too small, pick out 3", replace only the square, and resew.

(Project 10, Kelly's Sweetheart Quilt, continued from page 34)

2. Sew strips together.

a. Sew Light A strips to the Pink B strips, making 10 sets. Use white or the lightest possible fabrics for this step. Press toward the dark.

b. Sew Pink A strips to the Light B strips, again making 10 sets and pressing toward the dark.

3. Cut cross-sections.

a. Lay out pairs of strips, right sides together.

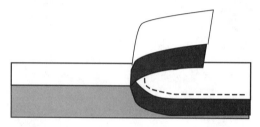

b. Cut 1-3/4" cross-sections, 12 from each pair. Keep them stacked neatly ready to sew together.

Tip: You don't need to cut all of the sections right now. It's your quilt and you're sewing for fun, so skip around from step to step all you wish. Cut about four other sets into cross-sections, start assembling blocks, then come back and cut more sections later

4. Sew pairs together. Keep sections aligned as they were when you cut them, and keep the large light area on top every time. Chain them together like this, and sew them with scant 1/4" seams:
Press sets open.

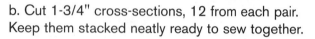

5. Add pink C strips.

a. Choose the longest 1-3/4" Pink strips. They must be a full 22" long (use the skimpy ones later).

b. Sew five pieced sets to each Pink strip, choosing a variety of different color combinations each time. Butt them up close to each other and sew carefully so you can get five on each strip.

c. Cut blocks apart. Press them. Quality control: Make sure blocks are 4-1/4" square. Adjust future seams if they aren't square. Continue working on Steps 2, 3, 4, and 5 to make 120 blocks. (If you run out of strip-pieced sections, make a few more.)

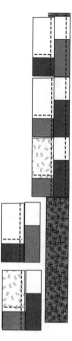

6. Make solid Pink blocks.

a. Sew remaining Pink strips together in sets of three, mixing up colors for a nice variety. Make sure sets are 4-1/4" wide.

b. Cut into 4-1/4" blocks. Make 30 blocks. If you run short, cut small pieces (1-3/4" x 4-1/4") and assemble more blocks.

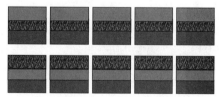

7. Make 102 solid Light blocks.

a. Sew light A strips together in 21 sets of three, again mixing up fabrics to create many different combinations. Press toward center strips.

b. Cut into 4-1/4" blocks. Cut carefully to get five if possible (you may get only four from some sets).

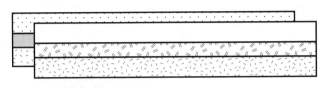

8. Begin assembling the quilt top.

a. Make 15 hearts, using eight Woodpile blocks, two solid Dark and two solid Light each time.

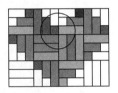

Tip: At some points, seams in adjacent blocks must line up. The circled area is the most important spot. Choose your best blocks and assemble 15 pairs like this first thing, keeping some contrast between the two Pink fabrics which touch.

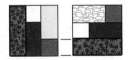

b. Join light blocks four at a time like this:

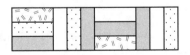

9. Complete the quilt top.

a. Make three vertical rows of five hearts and six sets of Light blocks, following the diagram at the right.

b. Join rows to make the quilt top.

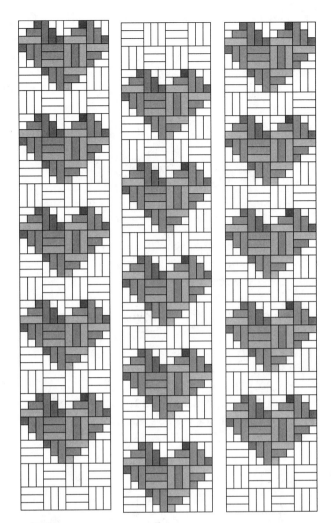

10. Add borders.

a. Cut seven strips 1-3/4" x 44" of light fabric. Piece them together to fit the sides, then top and bottom.

b. Cut pink borders. If only one border is used, make it about 5" wide. If two, make the inner one about 2-1/2", the outer one about 3". (Or use any desired widths.)

11. Quilt and bind with your favorite methods. The quilt on page 34 shows one quilting pattern, which repeats the heart shapes in both the pink and the light areas. It's more time-consuming than stippling or random patterns, but it makes the design stand out better.

(Project 11, Fancy Paths, continued from page 38)

4. Cut 2" sections from the first set. You need 18 sections. Stack them neatly for sewing without rearranging.

5. Complete the first set of 18 blocks.
a. Sew pairs together with a scant 1/4" seam, chaining as shown. Keep the largest light area on top. Press toward the dark fabric.
b. Make a test block by sewing one pair to a 2" x 5" strip of the C fabric. Measure to make sure the block is 5" square. (There is no allowance for trimming this time.) Adjust seams if necessary to complete the remaining blocks.
c. Sew six pairs to each C strip (2" x 44") strip. Refer to your mock-up blocks to make sure you have the correct color! Save ends of strips for Step 7.

d. Cut blocks apart, using a small grid to keep them square. Press toward the dark.

6. Repeat Steps 4 and 5 to make 18 blocks from the other color scheme.

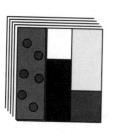

7. Add triangles.
a. Cut 36 2" squares, 18 of each color. (Stack the ends of the strips from Step 5b and cut several at a time.)
b. Sew contrasting squares to the dark corners of each block, chaining like this:
c. Trim and press to make triangles.

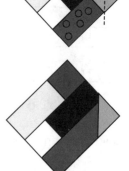

8. Sew blocks together.
a. Join in sets of four. Notice where the colors go.
b. Combine nine sets to make the quilt top.

9. Add borders.
a. Cut 2" borders of light fabric and add them.
b. Add 3" borders of dark fabric.
10. Quilt and bind with your favorite methods.

(Project 12, Toasted Triangles, continued from page 38)

4. Cut 200 Red squares.
a. Cut ten 2" x 41" strips of Red fabric.
b. Cut each strip into 20 squares. (Stack five strips, cut them into squares, then stack the remaining five and cut them into squares.)

5. Add triangles (see page 37).
a. Sew squares to strips like this, at the same angle:
b. Trim seams.
c. Press to form triangles. (Press seams toward the center.)

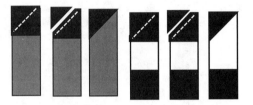

No need to add triangles to all pieces right now. Do a few, go on to Step 6 and finish up some blocks, then come back to Step 5. You're sewing for fun, so skip around as much as you want.

6. Assemble blocks. There is no allowance for trimming this time, so make a test block to be sure the blocks will be 5" square, and make sure ends are lined up evenly. Don't get careless—lots of things have to line up in Step 7! Check blocks for accuracy as you go and you'll save yourself a lot of seam-ripping later. All of these measurements must be exactly 1-3/4".

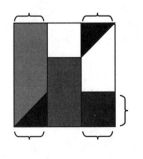

7. Combine small blocks into 20 large blocks.

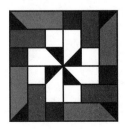

8. Sew all blocks together.
9. Make pieced borders.
a. Cut 18 strips 2" x 8" of the fabric used for Dark C (or any fabric you prefer).
b. Add triangles as in Step 5.
c. Make 22 sets of triangles like this: (Do Stitch and Flip, sewing 22 Red squares to squares of the fabric in Steps A and B. Or use any other method for making triangle sets exactly 2" square.)
d. Assemble a few units to make sure seams will line up with quilt blocks.
e. Add borders following the diagram. The extra four sets of triangles go in the corners.

10. Add additional borders if desired.
11. Quilt and bind with your favorite method.

(Project 13, Housewarming, continued from page 39)

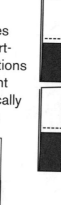

5. Sew pairs together. Sew only the ones paired off right sides together with a partner. Use scant 1/4" seam, chaining sections together as shown. Keep the largest light section on top and blocks will automatically slant the right way. Make 36 sets. Press toward the darker section.

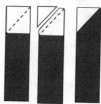

6. Cut 2" squares, 36 Dark and 36 Light or Bright (later you'll cut more for borders).

7. Add triangles.

a. Sew Dark squares to Light strips as shown (see page 37 for more information). Trim and press back to make triangles.

b. Sew light or bright squares to solid dark strips. The seams go at the same angle as before. Press toward the dark.

8. Assemble blocks.

a. Make a test block. Press it and see if it is 6-1/2" square. If it isn't, repair it and make final seams a little wider or narrower in future blocks.

b. Make 36 blocks.

9. Assemble the quilt top. Be careful to keep points accurate where eight seams meet.

a. Make sets of four blocks.

b. Assemble nine sets to make the quilt top.

10. Add pieced borders.

a. Cut 12 2" x 11" strips of dark fabric.

b. Cut 2" squares:

16 of dark (border color)

28 of bright (color of triangles on edge of quilt)

c. Use Stitch and Flip technique to make triangles.

d. Assemble triangles like this (12 long sets, four extras):

Make 12 of these.   Make four of these.

e. Baste together, adjust to fit, reinforce seams, and sew to the quilt.

11. Add outer borders. Add a 4" plaid border, if desired. Lois's quilt has dark squares in the corners.

12. Quilt and bind with your favorite method.

(Project 14, Glowing Pinwheels, continued from page 40)

1. Cut 42 strips (two of each fabric):
(Refer to the mock-up block; match A, B, C, D)

All A fabrics (total of 12 strips)	2" x 44"
All B fabrics (total of 12 strips)	3-1/2" x 44"
All C fabrics (total of 12 strips)	5" x 44"
All D fabrics (total of six strips)	6-1/2" x 44"

Tip: If using fat quarters: Use four strips of each at least 21" long. You'll need a total of 84 strips!

2. Sew strips together for Green blocks. Set aside the widest dark strips (D strips) because they have no partners. Sew the others together like this, using scant 1/4" seams: Press toward the dark.

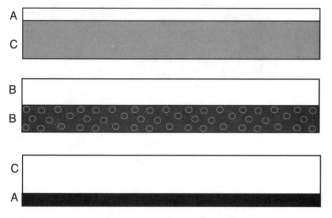

3. Lay out panels and cut cross-sections.
a. Lay out the A/C panel (mostly dark, just a little light) and the B/B panel (half dark, half light). Have right sides together and dark edges together, neatly aligned.

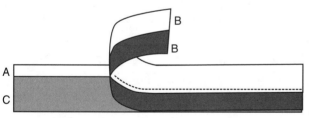

b. Cut 2" sections (you'll need 40). Leave them stacked neatly like this, lighter side up, ready to sew.

4. Sew these sets together. Keep the larger light area on top as shown in the art. Use scant 1/4" seams and line up ends neatly. Cut apart. Press toward the darker areas and set aside. All sections must be identical.

> It's okay to work ahead… Eager to see finished blocks? Do about eight units, work ahead to Step 9, then come back and finish remaining blocks.

5. Arrange remaining panels and cut 2" cross-sections. Stack identical panels, right side up. Cut 2" sections and stack them neatly. You'll need 40 of each.

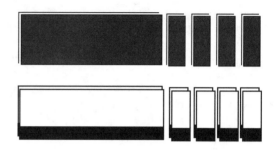

6. Cut 2" squares for Stitch and Flip. Cut the gold fabric into 10 strips 2" x 44". Stack the strips and cut into 200 squares, 20 from each strip.

7. Add gold triangles.
a. On each Light strip, sew a square to the opposite end from the dark square. Make sure seams all go the same way! Trim seams, fold back, and press.

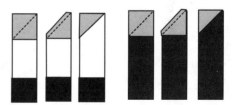

b. Repeat, sewing a square to only 27 of the Dark strips, at the same angle.

8. Make a test block.
a. Assemble one block like this: Press it and measure it. It should be 6-1/2" square. If it isn't, make the final seams a little wider or narrower. The small dark square (arrow) must be 1-3/4" square so seams will line up in adjoining blocks.

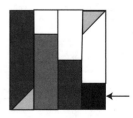

(Glowing Pinwheels, continued)

b. Make 27 blocks with two triangles, 13 blocks with only one. Continue to monitor accuracy so blocks are 6-1/2" square. Press toward the darker side of the blocks.

9. Repeat Steps 2 to 7 to make 40 Navy blocks. Make 28 blocks with two triangles, 12 blocks with one.

10. Make 40 Red blocks. Make 25 blocks with two triangles, 15 blocks with one.

11. Arrange blocks in rows. Use this diagram to keep track of where the colors go:

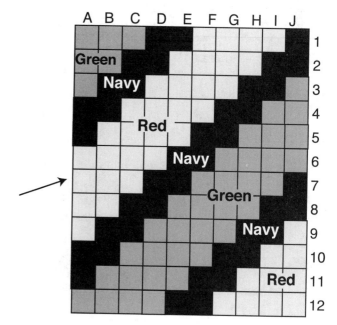

This step is quite tricky. You also need to arrange blocks into this pattern and you must keep track of which blocks have two triangles and which have only one.

Because there are no triangles on the outer edges of the quilt, I suggest you lay out all the one-triangle blocks first. Fill in the center with two-triangle blocks. When you are sure the arrangement is correct, pin blocks in 12 rows of 10 blocks.

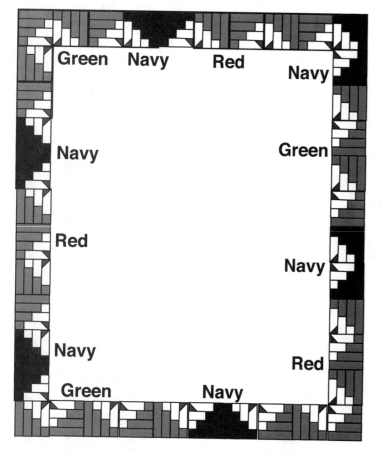

Label the blocks and stack them methodically because it will be quite time-consuming to complete the quilt top. You probably can't leave the layout spread out on your floor that long.

12. Sew rows together. Not only must the seams of the small dark squares line up with seams in adjacent blocks, but seams of eight triangles must come together. If you were accurate in making the blocks, here's where it pays off.

13. Quilt and bind as desired. Betty's project was quilted on a commercial machine with a wobbling stitch that followed the design lines.

Design-Your-Own

Stitch and Flip Triangles, Three Steps

Standard

Alternate

Block size (after seams)	3-3/4" Normal	4-1/2" Large		
Step height	1-1/4"	1-1/2"		
Dark C	4-1/4"	5"	Light C	
Light A	1-3/4"	2"	Dark A	
Dark B	3"	3-1/2"	Light B	
Light B	3"	3-1/2"	Dark B	
Dark A	1-3/4"	2"	Light A	
Cut sections this wide	1-3/4"	2"		

Note: Mini and Small sizes are not recommended for this technique.

Squares which will become triangles are also cut this size

Mock-up Blocks

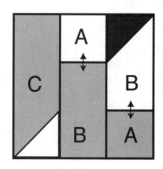

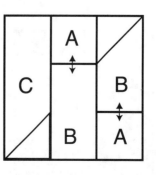

Stitch and Flip Triangles, Four Steps

Standard

Does not include 1/4" allowance for trimming.

Alternate

Note: Mini and Small sizes are not recommended for this technique.

Block size (after seams)	5" Normal	6" Large		
Step height	1-1/4"	1-1/2"		
Dark [D]	5-1/2"	6-1/2"	Light [D]	
Light [A]	1-3/4"	2"	Dark [A]	
Dark [C]	4-1/4"	5"	Light [C]	
Light [B]	3"	3-1/2"	Dark [B]	
Dark [B]	3"	3-1/2"	Light [B]	
Light [C]	4-1/4"	5"	Dark [C]	
Dark [A]	1-3/4"	2"	Light [A]	
Cut sections this wide	1-3/4"	2"		

Squares which will become triangles are also cut this size

Mock-up Blocks

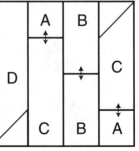

Part 2 • Reverse Blocks

All of the projects in the first half of the book were made with Regular blocks with steps going down like this:

There are dozens of arrangements you can make. There are even more design effects you can get if part of the blocks have steps going up like this:

I call them Reverse blocks. In the artwork I put a dot on the Reverse blocks so you can identify them.

Almost all of the projects in the last half of the book have some Reverse blocks. (None use all Reverse blocks— the design effect would be the same as all Regular. If you accidentally make all blocks Reverse, use designs from the first half of the book, mentally reversing the art- work or looking at it in a mirror.)

Quilt made by Gloria Pritchett of Issaquah, Washington.

Design Effects with Reverse Blocks Added

The most important design effect is this one, which is used for the popular Barn Raising and Straight Furrows designs:

Right: Betsy Hallock Heath of Cheshire, Massachusetts, used a scenic print for the background of "Adobe Steps," a variation of Project 15.

How to Make Reverse Blocks

Regular Blocks

When making any project in the first half of the book, you keep the cross-sections stacked so the pieces on top have larger light areas. When the seams are sewn and the blocks opened up, steps go down.

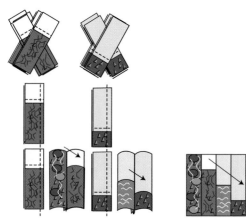

Reverse Blocks

Turn over the stacks. The larger dark sections are now on top. When you sew the seams and open up the blocks, they look like this, with steps going up:

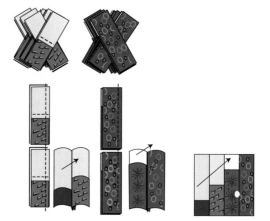

Blocks can be turned to look like this:

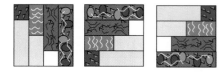

Blocks can be turned to look like this:

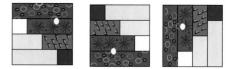

Although Regular blocks are versatile enough for dozens of layouts, they don't work in every situation. Darks might be in the right place, but seams might go the wrong way. Reverse blocks solve the problem. By using both types, you can have seams going whichever direction you need and the darks and lights where you need them.

Lois Stoltenburg, of Chehalis, Washington, started this beautiful quilt in a class at the Something to Crow About shop in Springfield, Oregon. The design circling the center suggested ripples in a pond, so she designed a border to suggest reeds along the bank. Appliquéd lily pads and a three-dimensional dragon fly pin complete the effect.

Double Your Designs
Project 15 • Kachina

With its simple arrangement and plain blocks separating pieced blocks, this might be the easiest project in the book. Original specifications were for "Southwestern" colors, but you can take liberties with that guideline, as did Christine Kamon of West Chester, Pennsylvania, who got a dramatic look with her exquisite fabrics. For much different examples, see pages 89, 92, and the back cover.

Make two mock-up blocks (pages 12 and 18)

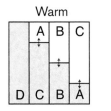

Warm   Cool

Fabric

Light (enough for blocks, background squares and borders): 1-2/3 yard
Inner border (blocks too): 1/3 yard
Outer border (blocks too): 7/8 yard
Single strips: 2" to 6" wide of six other dark fabrics (see Step 1)
Optional: Strips of six other light fabrics (see Step 1)
Lining: 3 yards (or as little as 1-1/2 yards if narrower borders are used)

> **Important:** Use the cutting layout on page 117 for cutting the background fabric, especially if you'll use that same color as the Light in all blocks.

Quilt size: 48" x 59"
Block size: 5"
Normal scale, four steps
Make 32 blocks, plus three Special blocks:

17 "Warm" blocks:
    Eight Regular   Eight Reverse   One Special

18 "Cool" blocks:
    Eight Regular   Eight Reverse   Two Special

   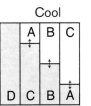 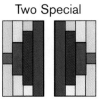

1. Cut 14 strips, then cut parts for Special blocks from scraps.*

Four A fabrics:
One strip 2" x 30" of each (two Dark, two Light)
Pieces for Special blocks: Two 1-3/4" squares of each Dark
    Eight 1-3/4" squares of Light (four of each, if two fabrics used)

Four B fabrics:
One strip 3-1/4" x 30" of each (two Dark, two Light)
Pieces for Special blocks: Two 1-3/4" x 4-1/4" of each Dark
    Eight 1-3/4" x 3-1/4" of Light (four of each, if two fabrics)

Four C fabrics:
One strip 4-1/2" x 30" of each (two Dark, two Light)
Pieces for Special blocks: Two 1-3/4" x 6-3/4" of each Dark
    Eight 1-3/4" x 4-1/2" of Light (four of each, if two fabrics)

Two D fabrics:
One strip 6" x 26" strip of each (two Dark)
Pieces for Special blocks: Two 1-3/4" x 10" of Cool color
    One 1-3/4" x 10" of Warm color

*Using a directional fabric? Cut parts for the Special blocks at Step 9 when you know which way the design should go!

(Project 15 continued on page 116)

Mr. and Mrs. Woodpile—A Variation of Project 15

Nan Tischler of Downingtown, Pennsylvania, made this imaginative queen-size quilt for her son and daughter-in-law, who both love the outdoors. Using fish and woodsy fabrics saved for years, Nan appliquéd in the borders a variety of critters: Mr. and Mrs. Deer, Mrs. and Mrs. Moose, and Mr. and Mrs. Bear. At the top is the newly-wed Mr. and Mrs. Tischler's home.

How to Arrange a Straight Furrows Design

Straight Furrows is a traditional name used since pioneer days for a very useful design which can be used for almost any size of quilt. Here's how to assemble Straight Furrows:

1. Make basically half Regular, half Reverse blocks. (If an odd number is used, make one more Regular.)

2. Keep each type of block stacked separately. (There are four stacks this time because there are both Regular and Reverse blocks from two different colors. You might have only two stacks.)

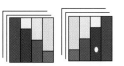
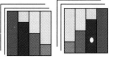

3. Lay out all of the Regular blocks, all turned the same way, in a checkerboard pattern (17 of one color, 18 of one color).

4. Fill in the spaces between blocks with Reverse blocks. Turn them on their sides with the darks in the same positions. If Straight Furrows isn't exciting enough for you, see pages 114 and 132 for some ways to make it sizzle.

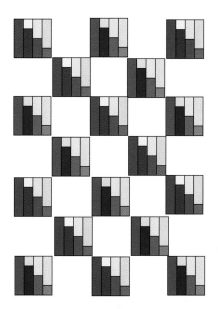

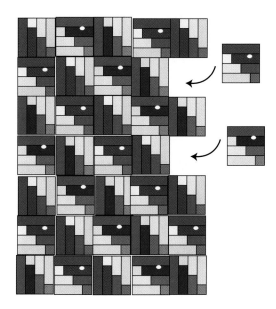

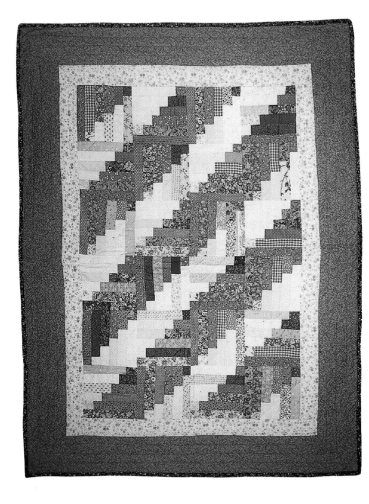

I made this little quilt for my granddaughter, Caitlyn Lemmon, when she was born. For a delicate baby quilt I used 24 blocks, small scale, six steps. Notice that the furrows can go either direction.

Project 16 • Rainbow Hearts

This quilt has Regular blocks alternating with Reverse in the Straight Furrows arrangement. Colors within each block merge through the colors of the rainbow, ending with little hearts. It was designed and made by Betsy Hallock Heath of Cheshire, Massachusetts.

Quilt size: 40" x 56"
Block size: 6"
Size: Small, six steps
Make 48 blocks

24 Regular   24 Reverse

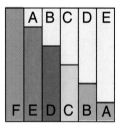

Fabric

Light: 1-1/4"
Pink: 1/3 yard (A and B)
Yellow: 1/4 yard (C)
Green: 1/3 yard (D)
Blue: 7/8 yard (E, plus borders)
Violet: 1/2 yard
Lining: 1-3/4 yards

The mock-up block is optional. You can use this diagram if your colors match.

1. Cut strips, cut two of each size:
Light:

      A = 1-3/4" x 44"
      B = 2-3/4" x 44"
      C = 3-3/4" x 44"
      D = 4-3/4" x 44"
      E = 5-3/4" x 44"
Pink A = 1-3/4" x 44"
Pink B = 2-3/4" x 44"
Yellow C = 3-3/4" x 44"
Green D = 4-3/4" x 44"
Blue E = 5-3/4" x 44"
Violet F = 7" x 44"

2. Sew strips together. Press toward the dark.

3. Lay out panels right sides together for cutting sections.

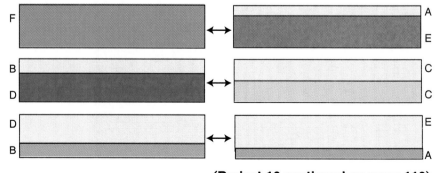

(Project 16 continued on page 118)

How to Arrange a Barn Raising Design

Designs that circle the center are very comforting and satisfying. Here's the most popular traditional arrangement, Barn Raising. Arranging the blocks is easy if you do it like this:

1. Make multiples of four blocks, half Regular and half Reverse blocks (usually). If making 36 blocks, make 20 Regular and 18 Reverse. If making 100 blocks, make 52 Regular and 48 Reverse. Keep each different type of block stacked separately.

2. Lay out pieces of yarn to show the four quarters of the quilt.

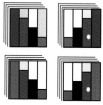

3. Start with four Regular blocks in the middle.

4. Add more Regular blocks. Use a second color scheme if you have one.

5. Make another diagonal row, still using only Regular blocks. Use a third color, or repeat the first one.

6. Continue building up the pattern. Within each quadrant, all blocks are turned the same direction.

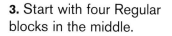

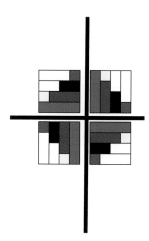

7. Fill in spaces with Reverse blocks (with dots). Place darks next to the darks, lights next to lights. Seams go the opposite direction from seams in Regular blocks already in place. All Reverse blocks in each section face the same direction. After the pattern is in place, you may choose to rotate some blocks to break it up. See Projects 19 and 20 and sketches on pages 114 and 132.

8. Try other color arrangements. Here are the same blocks with colors arranged differently.

Project 17 • Barn Raising

I think this is was my first Woodpile quilt, made for my 1991 book, *Scrap Quilts Using Fast Patch*, as an alternative to Log Cabin Quilts. Before starting, see pages 32, 75, and 76 for suggestions for making scrap quilts.

Quilt size: About 64" x 82"
Block size: 9" square
Size: Large, six steps
Make 48 blocks with randomly mixed fabrics:

24 Regular   24 Reverse

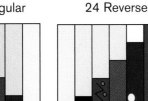

No mock-up blocks are needed.

Fabric

Dark fabrics:
    10 fat quarters*
    About 15 to 20 long scraps at least 2" wide
Light fabrics:
    10 fat quarters*
    Inner borders: 3/8 yard
    Outer borders: 1 yard
Lining: 4 to 5 yards
*I say to use fat quarters to simplify buying and cutting fabric. Scraps make a prettier quilt, especially if you choose more fabrics as you go.

1. Cut strips
a. Stack five Dark fat quarters evenly and cut these strips (five of each size):
        A = 2-1/4" x 21"
        C = 5-1/4" x 21"
        E = 8-1/4" x 21"
b. Stack five more Dark fat quarters and cut these strips (five of each size):
        B = 3-3/4" x 21"
        D = 6-3/4" x 21"
c. Trim the long Dark scraps to 2" x 10". You will eventually need 48, but cut some of them later when you see which colors you need more of. (You can use leftovers from the above steps if you wish, but the effect is prettier if you avoid repeating fabrics.)

d. Stack five Light fat quarters and cut these strips (five of each size):
        A = 2-1/4" x 21"
        C = 5-1/4" x 21"
        E = 8-1/4" x 21"
e. Stack five more Light fat quarters and cut these strips (five of each size):
        B = 3-3/4" x 21"
        D = 6-3/4" x 21"
Note: Set aside leftovers promptly so they don't get mixed up with your official strips!

(Project 17 continued on page 119)

Adventures with 100 Blocks

While developing ideas for this book, I decided to try all of the layouts in my book, *Scrap Quilts Using Fast Patch*. It gives about 40 layouts suitable for any diagonally divided block, such as Log Cabin and Woodpile. Nobody, including me, could tell how many Regular and Reverse blocks some of the layouts needed. So I made 100 blocks, 50 Regular and 50 Reverse, spread them out in one layout after another, and took photographs until I ran out of film. Here are some of the things I discovered:

1. With experience, you can predict by looking at a layout whether it uses Regular blocks only or both Regular and Reverse. See page 113 for the general patterns formed.

2. If you want to make up a design as you go along, sew half the total number of blocks you expect to use—all Regular because every design has at least half Regular and many use no Reverse blocks. Lay out half of the quilt and decide how many of each type you need to finish it.

3. When laying out your half-quilt, visualize Reverse blocks by turning Regular blocks over so seams are up. This makes darks and lights go the opposite way. Here's one of my snapshots to show what I mean. Count up all of the wrong-side-up blocks you have in your half-quilt and multiply by two and you'll see how many Reverse you need for the whole quilt. Make the rest Regular.

4. Designs with 36 or 100 blocks are special. With a design which usually takes half Regular and half Reverse, such as a variation of Barn Raising, count how many blocks of each type are in each quadrant and multiply by four. The 100-block layout on the right has 25 blocks in each quadrant, 13 Regular and 12 Reverse, so the total is 52 Regular and 48 Reverse. I sewed two more Regular blocks and removed two Reverse blocks. Then I made four 25-block quilts.

Straight Furrows really does take half and half, unless an odd number of blocks is used (then you'd use one more Regular). The 25-block quilts can't be combined into Straight Furrows (left).

This 100-block experiment is continued in Project 18 on the next page.

Project 18 • Before and After

The 100 blocks on the previous page were made into four quilts of 25 blocks each. Then those were cut apart diagonally and combined into two medium-sized quilts, with darks and lights in opposite positions.

Quilt size: Two quilts about 54" square before borders
Block size: 7-1/2" square
Normal size, six steps

Total blocks: 100

52 Regular   48 Reverse

Fabric

A wide variety of scraps. See Step 1 on page 120. Plan on adding new fabrics after most of the blocks are made. (I decided half-way through that my blocks were crying out for plaids, so I added a lot of them.)
Lining: Match the quilt top and add 2" each way
I made a pieced lining for my quilt, starting with a 44" square, then adding a 6" border to each side.

Make 100 blocks as directed on page 120. Make four quilts of 25 blocks, with Regular and Reverse blocks in the same position in each. See pages 93 and 95.
Cut diagonally through each just inside the light area as shown on the left. Practice on a paper version from page 122 first.
Combine the parts into two quilts.

(Project 18 continued on page 120)

More Design Ideas for Reverse Blocks

On pages 20 and 21, I showed how designs often started with circle or Pinwheel centers. We still use those when Reverse blocks are added. (Barn Raising has a circle in the center, as you noticed). Here I took those same loose blocks and added some Reverse and went back to the flannelboard. I used 64 blocks; two sets of 16 blocks were Regular and two sets of 16 were Reverse.

1. Start with a circle, build it up like Barn Raising, then rotate some blocks to break up the pattern. Or look at it this way: Start with a 16-block design and add a border of blocks (see pages 124 and 125).

2. Start with a 16-block Pinwheel, also from page 123. Add a border of blocks from page 124. Notice that 36-block designs usually have 20 Regular and 16 Reverse blocks (count the blocks in one quadrant and multiply by four).

Short on blocks? Plain blocks are often substituted for Woodpile blocks, usually in the corners.

3. Start with a 16-block design from page 123 or 127. Repeat it four times. You create secondary patterns where the corners come together.

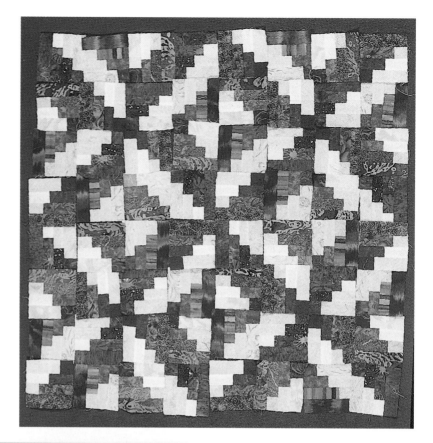

Here's the way I finally sewed the blocks together, another set of four 16-block designs. (This might be set on point. Tilt the page and see what I mean.)

Project 19 • Cozy Quilt

As a general rule, the most satisfying Woodpile quilts have blocks with several different color schemes arranged in a balanced way. For this pretty Barn Raising variation, Marilyn Roland of Woodland, California, used a beautiful array of batik and color wash fabrics.

Quilt size: 38" x 46"
Block size: 5" square
Normal size, four steps
Total blocks: 48

12 Regular 12 Regular 12 Reverse 12 Reverse

Make four mock-up blocks (pages 12, 18, and 150), one for each color scheme.

Fabric

28 strips, each 22" long (see Step 1)
16 Darks (all different) 2" to 6" wide
12 Lights (all different or you can repeat any colors) 2" to 6" wide
Border: 1/2 yard
Lining: 1-1/2 yards

1. Cut strips, with mock-up blocks as a guide.

Four Darks	Four Lights
A = 2" x 22"	2" x 22"
B = 3-1/4" x 44"	3-1/4" x 44"
C = 4-1/2" x 44"	4-1/2" x 44"
D = 6" x 44"	

2. Sew in pairs, following your mock-up blocks.
3. Lay out the first color combination like this, keeping right sides together.

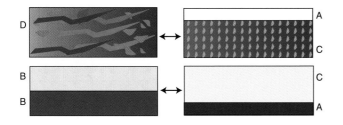

4. Cut 12 cross-sections 1-3/4" wide. Stack like this, keeping the largest light pieces on top.

(Project 19 continued on page 136)

Project 20 • Boca Barn Raising

This is a beautiful scrap quilt, but look closely; the scraps are not random. There are four sets of blocks, about 25 of each. It's usually quicker to make blocks in identical sets rather than mixing up parts in a random way. This Barn Raising variation was made by Zvia Strahilevitz-Klein of Boca Raton, Florida.

Quilt size: 60" square
Block size: 5"
Normal scale, four steps
Total blocks: 100

52 Regular   48 Reverse

Both Regular and Reverse blocks are in four different color schemes. Mockup blocks are optional (pages 12 and 18).

Fabric

Strips of 28 fabrics, plus a few scraps
Inner borders: 1/4 yard
Outer borders: 3/4 to 1 yard
Lining: 3-1/2 yards

1. Cut strips

Dark fabrics	Light fabrics
A = Four 2" x 44"	Four 2" x 44"
B = Four 3-1/4" x 44"	Four 3-1/4" x 44"
C = Four 4-1/2" x 44"	Four 4-1/2" x 44"
D = Four 6" x 44"	

(Plus a few scraps to make four more blocks; see Step 11.)

2. Sew together the first set of fabrics as shown below.

3. Pair off like this:

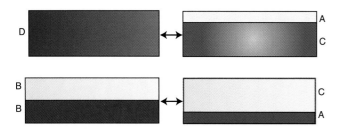

4. Cut 1-3/4" cross-sections. Stack like this, with larger light sections on top:

5. Sew 12 of the sets together. Use a scant 1/4" seam.

(Project 20 continued on page 137)

Project 21 • Pinwheel Stars

Here's another example of combining four 16-block designs, all made from a wide variety of scraps. (The sample uses green scraps for Regular blocks, purple scraps for Reverse.) Strips are 22" or less so you can use leftovers from your favorite fat quarters.

Quilt size: 62" square
Block size: 6-1/2"
Normal scale, five steps
Make 64 blocks, in two different color ways.

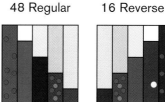

48 Regular   16 Reverse

Fabric

A variety of scraps (see Step 1)
1/3 yard for inner borders
1 yard for outer borders (use some for blocks)
4 yards lining
Batting
1/4 yard binding

Mock-up blocks are optional.

1. Cut 54 strips. For Regular blocks (Green), cut four of each size. Use many different fabrics for the darks; you can repeat lights:

Dark fabrics	Light fabrics
A = 2" x 22"	2-1/4" x 22"
B = 3-1/4" x 22"	3-1/4" x 22"
C = 4-1/2" x 22"	4-1/2" x 22"
D = 5-3/4" x 22"	5-3/4" x 22"
E = 7-1/4" x 22"	

(Alternate: For E, cut 48 pieces 1-3/4" x 7-1/4".)
For Reverse blocks (Purple), cut two of each:

Dark fabrics	Light fabrics
A = 2" x 15"*	2-1/4" x 15"
B = 3-1/4" x 15"	3-1/4" x 15"
C = 4-1/2" x 15"	4-1/2" x 15"
D = 5-3/4" x 15"	5-3/4" x 15"
E = 7-1/4" x 15"	

*Have a good contrast between the two Dark A strips for a nice effect in the center of the pinwheels. Other colors can be repeated if necessary.

2. Sew together strips for Regular blocks. Pair off as shown below. To avoid errors, pin the pairs and check to see if the widths add up to about 7".
3. Arrange strips for cutting cross-sections. Want an authentic scrap look? Stack strips as shown on page 76. That's how the sample quilt was made. In a hurry? Line up fabrics in pairs right sides together (below) so they'll be ready to sew together in Step 4.

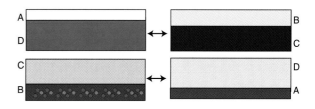

(Project 21 continued on page 138)

Project 22 • Tulips in the Woodpile

Diane Leighton, a nurse and quilt teacher of Yuba City, California, made this beautiful queen size scrap quilt for the 1995 Valley Quilt Guild Show. For those who are deprived of a rich supply of real scraps (or friends with real scraps to share), I have simplified the directions to use fat quarters. This is a big project; get together with friends or allow plenty of time to piece it for the most enjoyment.

Quilt size: 90" x 108"
Block size: 9" square
Size: Large, six steps
Make 120 blocks

84 Regular

36 Reverse

No mock-up blocks are needed.

Fabric

Dark fabrics: Dozens of scraps, or 25 fat quarters (buy some of them later), plus 20 to 30 long scraps at least 2" wide
Light fabrics: Dozens of scraps, or 25 fat quarters, or 1/2 yard pieces of 10 to 12 fabrics.
Lining: As much as 8 yards (you can use a bed sheet; don't try to hand-quilt it if a high thread count.)

1. Cut a starter supply of strips. Do not cut all of them now! Cut more when blocks are partly done and you see which colors you need more of. As you go along, you'll spot more fabrics you want to buy, and friends will contribute scraps.
Total strips needed eventually:
(If some are 21", not a full 22", that's okay)

Dark fabrics	Light fabrics
A = 12 strips 2-1/4" x 22"	12 strips 2-1/4" x 22"
B = 12 strips 3-3/4" x 22"	12 strips 3-3/4" x 22"
C = 12 strips 5-1/4" x 22"	12 strips 5-1/4" x 22"
D = 12 strips 6-3/4" x 22"	12 strips 6-3/4" x 22"
E = 12 strips 8-1/4" x 22"	12 strips 8-1/4" x 22"
F = 120 pieces 2" x 10"	

Starter supply:
a. Stack six or seven Dark fat quarters and cut these strips:

    A = 2-1/4" x 22"
    C = 5-1/4" x 22"
    E = 8-1/4" x 22"

b. Repeat that step with Light fat quarters.
c. Stack the same number of Dark fat quarters (or scraps at least 11" x 22") and cut these strips:

    B = 3-3/4" x 22"
    D = 6-3/4" x 22"

d. Repeat with Light fat quarters.
e. Cut dark scraps into 40 to 50 pieces, 2" x 10" (F).

(Project 22 continued on page 139)

Borders from Double Blocks

A simple idea that is very popular is to use double blocks as borders. This type is adjustable to fit the space available. (Make the border a tiny bit longer than you need, then widen some of the seams to shorten it until it is just right.) Here are some variations:

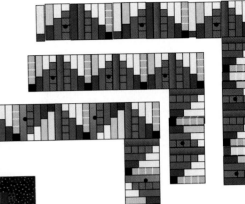

"A Kiss and a Promise"

Here's a work in progress (below). Jan Smith of Murrysville, Pennsylvania, used colors from her daughter Melissa's wallpaper and is making her a quilt. She promises to put another layer of borders around.

Put a Woodpile border around any quilt. Elaine Shephard of Mercer Island, Washington, used tiny Woodpile blocks around her Pine Tree wall hanging (below). (Can't decide what to do in the corners? Put something entirely different there, as Elaine did.)

Project 23 • Fireman's Fancy

At the Something to Crow About quilt shop in Springfield, Oregon, Teri Harter made this woodsy quilt for her son-in-law, a fireman who enjoys camping and hiking in the woods. Little accent squares separate the light and dark sides of each block and spiral across the quilt. Two background fabrics are used, but you can use a wide variety of fabrics for a scrappy look. Kris Bizzarri did the machine quilting.

Quilt size: 65" x 86"
Block size: 5"
Normal size, four steps
Total blocks: 96
24 of each type

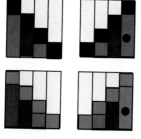
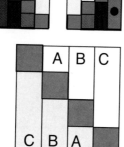

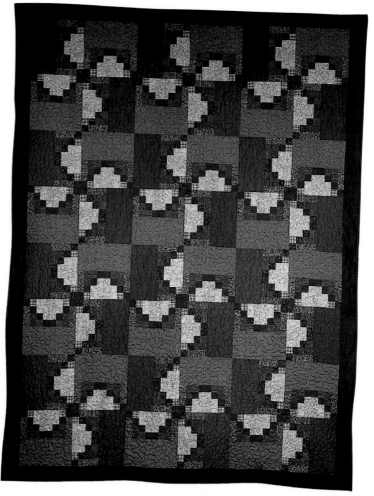

Make two mock-up blocks. Sketch your own diagrams like this:

Fabric

Dark fabrics	Light fabrics
A = 1/4 yard	1/4 yard
B = 3/8 yard	3/8 yard
C = 5/8 yard	1/3 yard of two fabrics

Red for accent squares: 1/3 yard
Black for accent squares: 1/3 yard
Backgrounds: 1-1/4 yards of two fabrics
Borders: About 1 yard
Lining: 4 yards

1. Cut strips

Dark fabrics	Light fabrics
A = Four 2" x 44"	Four 2" x 44"
B = Four 3-1/4" x 44"	Four 3-1/4" x 44"
C = Four 4-1/2" x 44"	Four 4-1/2" x 44"

(Cut Light C from two or more fabrics)
Red accent: Eight 1-3/4" x 44"
Black accent: Eight 1-3/4" x 44"

2. Sew strips together. Make four of each type, two with red strips and two with black. (Have two different Light C fabrics used with Reds, the same two or two new ones paired with Blacks.)
3. Arrange panels for cutting. Keep right sides together so cross-sections will be ready to sew.

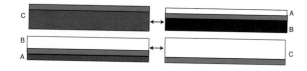

Fabric notes:
a. The directions called for "black," but Teri used dark brown. Feel free to make creative changes yourself.
b. Teri used only three light fabrics, but I suggest at least four (see Step 9).
c. Scrap fabrics work well. Just cut the total strips listed in Step 1.
d. If using fat quarters, make twice as many strips, 22" long.

(Project 23 continued on page 140)

Anita's Sketchbook

From the Cutting Room Floor

I generated a lot more ideas than I had time to sew or room to explain. If these ideas grab your attention, try them on your own.

Medallion Quilt

Bachelor's Puzzle

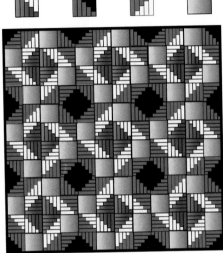

Hearts on Point

I didn't even have room for setting quilts on point. The general technique is in my book *Scrap Quilts Using Fast Patch*. See the Appendix for more information

Lovers? Not

For more ideas, check my web page.

Hot Idea: Make Shattered Blocks

Here's the quilt which inspired Woodpile blocks. It was designed by Carolyn Deevy of San Francisco, who got the idea from a painting by Mimi Vang Olson. It uses six-step blocks like this and took Carolyn and six friends two years to make.

Blocks have the light side broken up into squares (I call them "Shattered"). There were lots of seams to line up, so I simplified Woodpile blocks to use solid strips, making it much easier to make. But I did sketch out some projects using Shattered blocks. Because they are time consuming to make and rather hard to explain, I included only two, Fanning the Fire, Project 24, and the Irish Cabin Wall Hanging, Project 25. The quilt at the right would use five-step blocks like this:

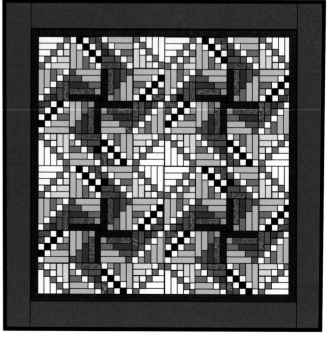

Sizzling 108 Quilts

Project 24 • Fanning the Fire

Lennie Honcoop of Elk Grove, California, put beautiful fabrics and workmanship into this quilt, as you can see from the close-up on the cover. Note: Although this project is at the end of the book it doesn't use Reverse blocks like the other projects in the second half of this book. It's here because it's more complex: Some blocks are shattered, and some have two dark colors instead of having a light and dark. (Shattered borders are optional; fabric allowances don't cover them.)

Quilt size: About 60" square
Block size: 6-1/4"
Normal scale, five steps
Total blocks: 64, all Regular

32 like this: 16 like this: 16 like this:

Make three mock-up blocks, page 12. (Mock-up blocks are not needed if your colors are similar.)

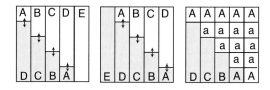

Fabric

Fat quarters:
> Seven Blue fat quarters
> Two "Drabs" (beige, gray, etc.)
> Six Red fat quarters
> Three Light fat quarters

Inner borders: 1/3 yard red
Outer borders: 3/4 or 1 yard
Lining: 3-1/2 yards

1. Cut strips as outlined on page 141. Sew Red/Blue strips together. Make four.

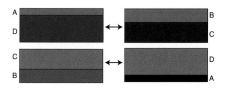

2. Sew Blue/Light strips together. (Caution: Don't use the narrowest Light (a) strips by accident for this step! Set them aside for Step 9.) Make two of each type.

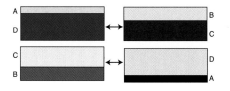

3. Lay out pairs to cut cross-sections, right sides together with the larger Light or Red sections on top.
4. Cut all pairs into 1-3/4" cross-sections. Stack as shown; keep the larger Light (or Red) on top.

5. Sew in pairs. Use a scant 1/4" seam.
6. Make a test block. Add the E strip. Press. Measure to make sure it is 6-3/4" wide.

(Project 24 cutting strategy is on page 141, step-by-step instructions are continued on page 142)

Project 25 • Irish Cabin

Here are two versions of the same wall hanging. Twelve blocks surround the center patchwork house, sharing the same dark strip in the center of each side. The black quilt was a prize winner made by Nancy Foisy of Coos Bay, Oregon, for the Sea and Surf Guild challenge to use black, white, and red fabric. The cabin in the center is surrounded with three-dimensional appliqué.

Pam Mennis of Norwich, New York, made a more colorful version. I'll base my directions on it because it's easier to see the construction in colors.

Quilt size: 29" square
Size of blocks: 6"
Small scale, six steps
Make 12 blocks

For a mock-up block, modify the six-step diagram on page 12. Cut 1/2" strips of A, B, C, D, E, and F, 1/2" squares of other colors.

Fabric

Scraps or strips cut from fat quarters are used for all parts of this project (see Step 1)
Lining: 1 yard

1. Cut 21 strips.
a. Cut one of each of these
   A = 1-3/4" x 22"
   B = 2-3/4" x 22"
   C = 3-3/4" x 22"
   D = 4-3/4" x 22"
   E = 5-3/4" x 22"
   F = 6-3/4" x 13" (only eight blocks need one)
b. Cut six strips 1-1/2" x 22" of White.
c. Cut three strips 1-1/2" x 22" of Red.
d. Cut six strips 1-1/2" x 22" of Medium (blue in Pam's).

2. Sew together as shown. Press away from the Light and away from the Red. For a quick start:

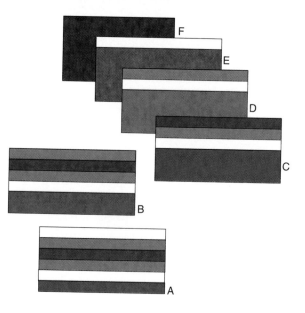

Tip: a. Sew a White strip to each Dark.
b. Sew a Medium to each Red.
c. Press these and you'll find it much easier to pin and sew all of the strips together.

(Project 25 continued on page 143)

Breaking the Rules

Doreen Clark of Mansfield, Massachusetts, got interested in quiltmaking just a few months ago, inspired by her mother, Cynthia Harris. The first block Cynthia taught her was Woodpile.

As you can see, Doreen already understands that written instructions are just to get you started. It's your fabric and your time, and you can turn your project into something quite different if you want to; I'll never know (unless you are kind enough to send me a photo of your results).

Doreen's Lighthouse

Fixing Mistakes

Often we are forced to be creative to save a project after we make a mistake. See pages 153 and 154 in the Appendix for ideas such as the one below, a way to save blocks that have been sewn together wrong.

Ignoring Mistakes

Lois Sanford of Margate, Florida, accidentally turned one block wrong when assembling this quilt for her new grandchild. She says, "I didn't notice [the error], but then it just makes the quilt's story a little more interesting, doesn't it? The important part of that quilt was in the story of how it got made. I met new friends, I had friends share their fabric... I had friends help put it together and quilt it, and no one noticed any 'mistake.' Maybe we all just looked at it with the same eye. It was a quilt for a grandchild made with love by friends. No one was thinking of looking for technical flaws. I quilt for the joy of it. It brought me joy. The quilt did its job and did it well."

Design-Your-Own

Celeste Delostrinos of Seattle, Washington, made this striking quilt at one of my Fast Patch Retreats on the Oregon Coast. She made curved blocks from her hand-dyed fabrics, using calculations from page 145. For accent, she added Stitch and Flip triangles, introduced on page 37. (No directions are included for this specific project.)

Review of Basic Types of Designs to Make with Regular and Reverse Blocks:

Regular Blocks Only

When only Regular blocks are used, you create zigzagging design lines like this: Look at designs in the first half of this book to see what I mean. The effect is the same if they are all Reverse blocks.

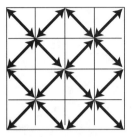

Regular Blocks Plus Plain Blocks

The zigzag pattern can be broken up by adding plain blocks. Project 3 (page 24) and Project 7 (page 30) are good examples of this.

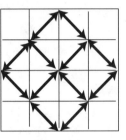
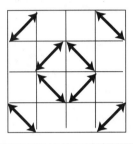

Half and Half

Arrangements that have diagonal patterns need an equal number of Regular and Reverse blocks. The most common use for diagonal lines is to have them circle the center. (Remember, 36- and 100-block arrangements aren't quite half and half.)

Instead of circling the center, the same parts can radiate from the center, but it's harder to come up with a good arrangement this way.

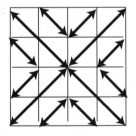

Odd Combinations

The most creative designs usually have Regular and Reverse in unequal numbers.

Plain blocks are often used, especially in the corners, for a more pleasing effect.

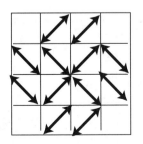
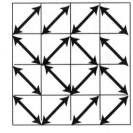
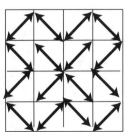

Overall Patterns—Basically Half Regular and Half Reverse

Fanciful arrangements are nice for wall hangings, but for a baby or bed quilt, you may prefer a simple overall pattern. For designs on these two pages, make half your blocks Regular, most of the others Reverse. Leave a few unassembled until you see which kind you need.

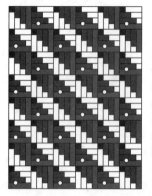

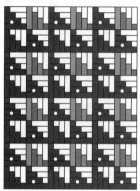

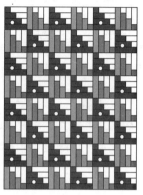

Plain Straight Furrows (page 93) works with any number of blocks vertically and any number horizontally. For a change, rotate some blocks or manipulate the color scheme (right). (Also see page 132.)

Good-old Barn Raising (see page 95) is also versatile, but it needs an even number of blocks vertically and an even number horizontally. (Remember 36- and 100-block quilts need four more Regular than Reverse.) For ways to vary this design, see pages 99, 101, 102, 125, and 132.

This can have any number of blocks vertically and any number horizontally. If there's an odd number vertically, use more Regular blocks than Reverse.

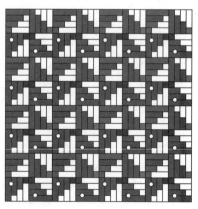

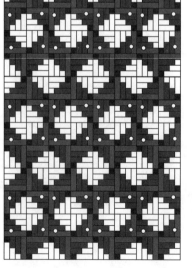

The arrangement on the left needs a multiple of four blocks vertically and an even number horizontally. Use smaller blocks and low-contrast fabrics for bold designs like this.

Be Prepared to Change Your Mind

You don't know until you lay out the finished blocks whether an arrangement will look good with the fabrics you chose. I almost always change my mind somewhat.

More Overall Patterns, Basically Half and Half

These quilts need an even number of blocks this ⟷ direction. If you follow that rule, you'll need half Regular and half Reverse blocks.

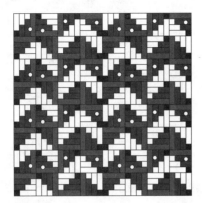

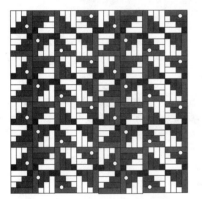
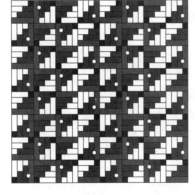
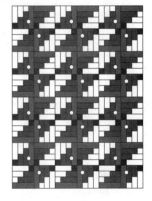

The designs below also need an even number of blocks ⟷ this direction. If there's an even number of blocks vertically, use half Regular and half Reverse. If there's an odd number, use more of one type than the other.

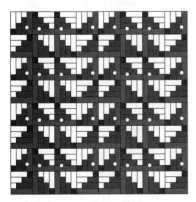

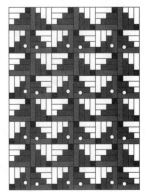

Remember that the simple view-finder described on page 42 can help you see what part of the design would look like.

(Project 15, Kachina, continued from page 91)

Set aside the pieces for the Special blocks.

2. Sew strips of Warm colors together, following your mock-up block. Press toward the darker colors.
3. Arrange strips in pairs for cutting sections. Have right sides together, dark fabrics along the same edge. (This piece is 4" shorter than the other.)
4. Lay out in pairs as shown. Cut 1-3/4" cross-sections, 16 of each.

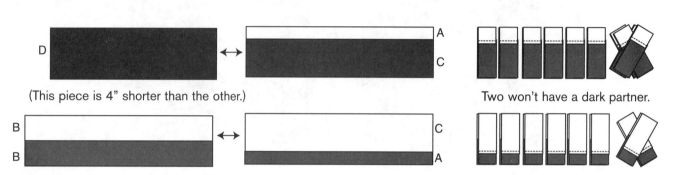

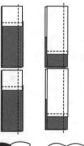

(This piece is 4" shorter than the other.)

Two won't have a dark partner.

5. Make eight Regular blocks.
a. Sew cross-sections together in pairs, keeping them turned the way they were stacked, with the largest light sections on top. Chain sections together as you sew for efficiency. Use a scant 1/4" seam.
b. Join sections to make blocks. The steps go down like this (arrow): (The test block made with other projects isn't needed this time. These blocks don't have to be perfectly square. Just keep them all a uniform height and uniform width.)
c. Trim off the top and bottom to square up blocks, page 15.
6. Repeat Steps 2 to 5 to make eight blocks with the Cool colors.

7. Make eight Reverse blocks from Warm colors.
a. Turn over the stacks of cross-sections.

b. Sew, keeping the largest dark areas on top this time.
c. When blocks are opened up, the steps go up like this:

8. Make eight Reverse blocks from Cool colors.

What about the missing dark strips?

Two blocks of each color scheme won't have D strips. (It doesn't matter whether they are Regular or Reverse blocks.) These blocks will be joined to whole blocks to make four double-wide blocks.

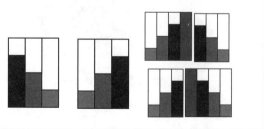

9. Make Special blocks.

a. Make double-wide blocks (box at the bottom of page 116) of both Warm and Cool colors.

b. Make two double tall blocks from Cool colors. Use the blocks you have already made as a guide and assemble the colors in the same order.

c. Make the double-wide and double-tall center block with Warm colors, again using the small blocks as a guide. Press toward the darks. Trim tops and bottoms evenly.

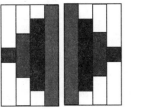

Note: The cutting layout at right shows how you could make best use of your background fabric if you want all light parts (pieced blocks, plain blocks, and borders) to be the same background fabric. If using directional fabric, take care to have the blocks go the right direction.

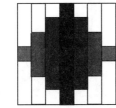

Cut pieces for Special blocks from scraps

Remove 8" for four 2" borders first.

A strips

B strips

C strips

Plain blocks

Double-tall | Double-wide

10. Cut plain blocks from background fabric.

a. Measure the small blocks and cut 24 blocks this size (about 5-1/2" square). If the height and width are not equal, label them to keep them turned the right direction.

b. Measure the double-wide blocks (should be about 9-1/4" x 5-1/2"). Cut four blocks that size.

c. Measure the double-tall blocks (about 5-1/2" x 9-1/4") and cut two blocks that size. Label them to avoid confusing them with the double-wide.

11. Assemble the quilt top.

a. Start at the center and combine blocks as shown.

b. Sew rows together, adjusting seams within blocks if necessary so blocks line up accurately.

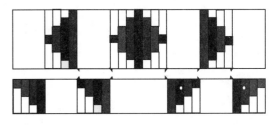

12. Add borders.

a. Add narrow inner borders, 1-3/4" or 2" wide from colored fabric or background fabric.

b. Add wide outer borders. These can be from 3" to 5" wide. You'll need five strips, if using 44" length.

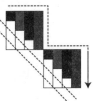

13. Quilt and bind with favorite methods. Christine machine-quilted hers entirely with vertical lines which followed the design and extended into the top and bottom borders too. You might also quilt with diagonal lines through the light area, supplemented with an outline of the dark side of the blocks.

(Project 16, Rainbow Hearts, continued from page 94)

4. Cut 1-1/2" cross-sections. Stack them like this with the larger light areas up. These colors will show: Blue, Yellow, Pink

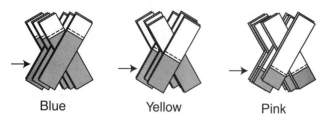

Blue   Yellow   Pink

5. Assemble 24 Regular blocks.
a. Keep Blue, Yellow, and Pink on top as you sew sections together.
b. Sew pairs into a test block to determine exactly how wide to make the seams. The block must be 6-1/2" wide.
c. Assemble 24 blocks with that seam width. Press toward the darks.
d. Trim blocks to 6-1/2" square, as shown on page 15. Make sure the small pink (A) squares are exactly 1-1/4" square.

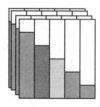

6. Turn over the stacks. These are the colors which show now: Violet, Green, Pink

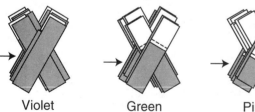

Violet   Green   Pink

7. Assemble 24 Reverse blocks. Repeat Step 5. Be sure to keep blocks 6-1/2" square and the small pink corners 1-1/4" square.

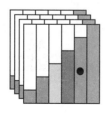

8. Arrange all of the Regular blocks like this:

9. Fill in the Reverse blocks. Line up the small pink squares with seams in neighboring blocks. (Seven squares on the edges don't have to line up, so use less accurate ones there.) Sew the quilt top together.

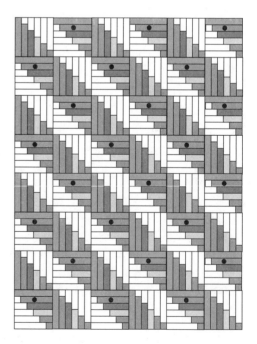

10. Add Blue borders (five strips 3" x 44").
11. Quilt and bind with your favorite methods. Quilt diagonally following the design, if you wish.

(Project 17, Barn Raising, continued from page 96)

2. Sew strips into panels. Pair off the 21" strips and sew them together. To avoid mistakes, pin them first and make sure the width of the two strips equals about 10".
Press toward the darks.

3. Cut cross-sections. With panels stacked as shown, cut all layers into 2" sections, 10 stacks from each set.

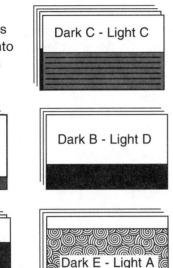

4. Make 24 Regular blocks.

a. Make a test block by sewing one of each type of section together, including a 2" x 10" (F) strip. Use a scant 1/4" seam. Keep the largest light sections on top with each seam and dark steps will automatically go down. Press toward the dark side and measure to see if the block is exactly 9-1/2" wide. Adjust future seams if necessary.

b. Assemble 24 blocks, following suggestions on page 46. Choose fabrics so all blocks are color coordinated and no two are alike.

c. Trim ends of blocks to 9-1/2" square. (Do not trim the sides!) The small dark square must be 1-3/4" square, so trim that end first (see page 15).

5. Make 24 Reverse blocks. This time, have the largest dark sections on top as you join parts so the steps go up. Continue to monitor seams so blocks are 9-1/2" wide.

Cut 2" x 10" strips of new fabrics as needed for a nice color effect in each block. (Add new colors in other parts of the blocks too, if you wish. Make 12 or 16 more blocks for a larger quilt, or save leftovers for a future quilt.)

6. Arrange blocks as shown on page 95. Mix up the colors for a nice balance. Try to keep a nice contrast between the dark end (F) strips and colors they touch (page 16).

Tip: In the photo on page 96, the center of the quilt has four Reverse blocks. Follow this artwork instead since it matches the directions on page 95. The effect will be basically the same.

7. Sew the quilt top together.

a. Join blocks, adjusting seams within blocks if needed so corners line up.

b. Add borders. To match art, cut seven strips 2" x 44" for inner borders and seven strips 5" x 44" for outer borders. Piece them to fit and sew in place.

8. Quilt and bind with your favorite methods. Commercial machine quilting which doesn't follow the design is fine. If quilting it myself, I sew diagonally, following the design, using light thread in the light parts, dark in the dark areas.

(Project 18, Before and After, continued from page 98)

1. Cut strips. These are directions for 22" strips. Use leftovers from fat quarters or cut them from 44" lengths.

Strips needed for 96 blocks. You need 100 blocks. To make up the shortage (and solve color problems and provide partners for "old maids"), add scraps of other fabrics when almost finished.

	Darks	Lights
A =	Eight strips 2" x 22"	Eight strips 2" x 22"
B =	Eight strips 3-1/4" x 22"	Eight strips 3-1/4" x 22"
C =	Eight strips 4-1/2" x 22"	Eight strips 4-1/2" x 22"
D =	Eight strips 5-3/4" x 22"	Eight strips 5-3/4" x 22"
E =	Eight strips 7" x 22"	Eight strips 7" x 22"
F =	100 strips 1-3/4" x 8-1/2"	

(Cut F pieces from long 1-3/4" scraps, as large a variety as possible. You can cut five from each 44" strip.)

Cutting suggestion: Make a starting supply from 24 fat quarters. This will give you almost half enough for the pieced panels and a few F pieces.

a. Choose 12 Light and 12 Dark fat quarters. Separate them by the size of the print (roughly; this isn't a firm rule).

b. Stack four Dark fat quarters at a time and cut as shown. If you use plaids or stripes, have them the top layer so you can cut along the lines somewhat. What about the F strips? If you don't have too many scraps on hand, cut some as shown in the layout (1-3/4" x 8-1/2"). You might even cut more of them from remnants of the other stacks, but see page 16. Most F pieces should be fabrics that are not used anywhere else to avoid arrangement problems. (I made up this rule after finishing my quilts.

I could not avoid "spines" and "long arms" because I repeated F fabrics too much in other parts of the quilt.)

c. Repeat with four light fat quarters cut the same sizes. Don't cut F pieces. Use remnants to cut some more of any other sizes.

Skimpy fat quarters? There is an extra inch or two in each layout to allow for aligning and trimming the first edge before cutting. If some pieces are too short (21" rather than 22"), use them anyway. If you can't cut enough cross-sections (Step 3), make up shortages from scraps.

Smallest prints	Medium size prints/plaids	Larger prints/plaids
A	B	D
A		
B	D	E
C		
C	E	F (maybe)

2. Sew strips together.

Light A - Dark E   Light B - Dark D   Light C - Dark C   Light D - Dark B   Light E - Dark A

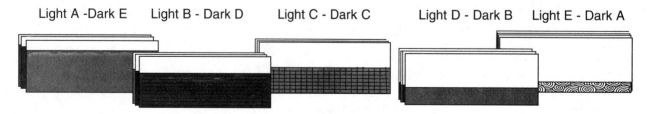

Try not to repeat the same combinations of fabrics in two panels. To avoid mistakes, pin each pair together, then check to see if the combined width is about 8-1/2".

3. Cut cross-sections. With panels stacked as shown in Step 2 (with like panels, right sides up, seams parallel but offset slightly to avoid bulk) cut through several layers at a time. If accuracy is an essential for you, cut only one layer at a time. Cut everything into 1-3/4" sections, 12 stacks from each set.

4. Make 52 Regular blocks—eventually.

a. Make a test block by sewing one of each type of section together, including an F strip. Use a scant 1/4" seam. Keep the largest light sections on top so steps will automatically go down. Press toward the dark side and measure to see if the block is exactly 8" wide. Adjust future seams if necessary.

b. Assemble as many blocks as you want now. Following suggestions on page 76, choose fabrics so all blocks are color coordinated and no two are alike. It's okay to skip ahead to Step 5, play with the finished blocks, then come back to Step 4. That helps you see if there are additional colors you might want to work in. Cut more strips from scraps or repeat the layouts with fat quarters on page 120.

c. Trim ends of blocks to 8" square. (Do not trim the sides!) The small dark square must be 1-1/2" square, so trim that end first. See page 15.

5. Make 48 Reverse blocks—eventually. This time, have the largest dark sections on top as you join parts so the steps go up. Continue to monitor seams so blocks are 8" wide, square with the small dark corner pieces 1-1/2" square.

6. Arrange blocks into rows of five. Mix up the colors for a nice balance. Keep a contrast with all of the colors the dark end strips touch (see page 16).

Make eight rows like this:

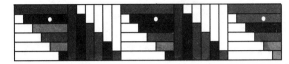

Make 12 rows like this:

7. Sew the rows into four 25-block quilts. Match the diagrams on page 122. Again, try to avoid unpleasant effects where the same colors touch, but some glitches are bound to happen at this stage. Look at the color photos throughout the book and you'll spot them. They make quilts more human.

Tip: A new place to hide mistakes: In other projects, if the dark A squares weren't quite square and wouldn't line up with neighbors, you could use them around the edges. Don't do that this time; the edges will be sewn together. Try the cut-apart exercise on page 122 to anticipate where you will cut in Step 8. Bury your mistakes along that line! Think about it (unless you don't make mistakes).

"A mind is a wonderful thing to change."

You're sewing for fun. This project won't be done overnight, so don't be surprised if you change your mind between the time you start and the time you finish. You might want to...

• Decide you are done at Step 7. Finish each quilt by adding lots of easy borders and make four lap robes for gifts to friends or nursing homes.

• Join all four quilts into one big Barn Raising quilt. See the photo on page 97. It will be about 80" square before borders.

• Make fewer blocks. If you don't think you have the scraps or the time to finish the project as planned, switch to any other arrangement in the book with fewer blocks—as long as you have the right number of Regular and Reverse blocks. If cross sections aren't sewn together, you can easily change your mind.

8. Stay stitch. Draw two lines where you will cut (see the diagrams below). Stay stitch along the light and dark edges. (The middle part with all of the seams will be discarded. It is still attached in the quilt on the floor on page 98).

9. Cut each panel apart. Cut 1/4" from the stitching. Sew all the top right corners into one quilt (the one on the piano in the photo on page 98.) Sew the bottom left corners into another quilt (the one on the floor).

10. Add borders, if you wish, of any desired width.

11. Quilt and bind with your favorite methods. Commercial machine quilting which doesn't follow the design is fine. I quilted mine on my regular machine. I used gently curving lines, with light thread in the light areas. I used straight lines with dark thread in the dark areas.

Practice with Paper

Before cutting your quilt tops apart (which requires a little courage), make a photocopy of these diagrams. Cut each one apart and tape the parts back together to try out the idea.

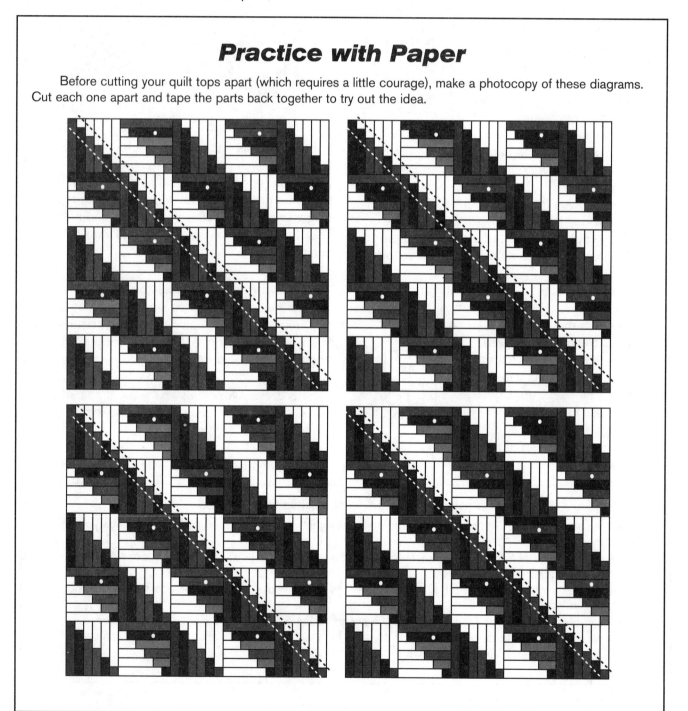

Arrangements for 16 Blocks (H/V)

Design options really increase when you add Reverse blocks. I can show only a few; find others on your own. These are "H/V" designs, which means that if you want to add borders from page 124, keep horizontal and vertical seams in the middle like this:

 Center Unit Uses Regular Blocks

 Center Unit Uses Reverse Blocks

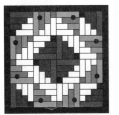 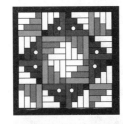 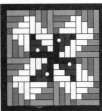 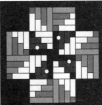

 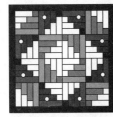  

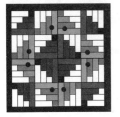 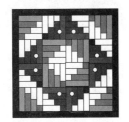 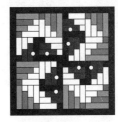  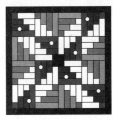

Same design, different colors

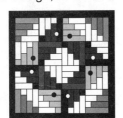 

Remember, your design can look quite different with other color arrangements. See Bachelor's Puzzle, page 107.

Asymmetrical Arrangements

If you're using only 16 blocks, use symmetrical designs. But if you plan to combine sets of 16 into larger quilts, try these (also see pages 100 and 103).

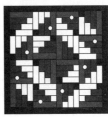 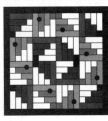

Borders with Reverse Blocks (for H/V Centers)

Use these for the 16-block arrangements on pages 44 and 123. (As always, these designs are just to get you started. You can alter any of them to suit your blocks, and you can design your own. I sketched out many other borders I didn't have room to include.)

Expand Your Quilt with More Borders

Start with a 16-block design from page 123 and add borders from page 124.

Design a border of blocks to create a 64-block quilt.

Add borders to the top and bottom only for an 80-block quilt.

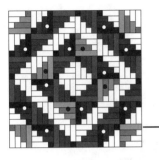

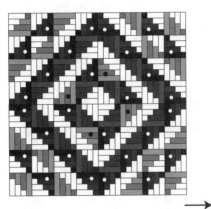

Here's another 16-block design from page 123 plus that same border from page 124. Add borders for a 64-block quilt.

Add borders to all sides for a 100-block quilt.

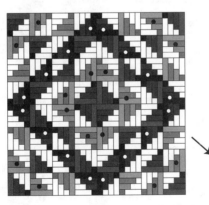

Designs on page 44 and borders on page 45 are interchangeable with these.

There are usually many different ways to distribute the colors. Don't assemble all blocks at once; things probably won't come out even. Instead, make part of the blocks and lay out part of the quilt. Turn blocks wrong side up temporarily to visualize and count (see page 97). Use a reducing glass (page 145) or just squint to check the visual effect. Determine how many more blocks of each color you need, and how many should be Regular and how many Reverse. If you want to duplicate a design I show, and I don't give you a breakdown, make your own tally sheet. Count the blocks of each type in each quadrant and multiply by four.

16-block Designs Combined to Make 64-block Quilts

Here's how some of the 16-block arrangements on page 123 might be combined to make quilts with 64 blocks.

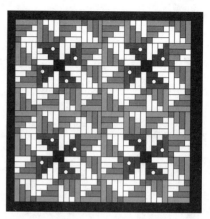

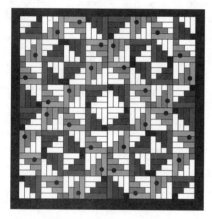

This one is special. The design was not symmetrical, so rotating the sections gives two quite different quilts.

Feel free to alter any design to fit your blocks. The quilt above uses 32 Reverse blocks; the one below uses only 16.

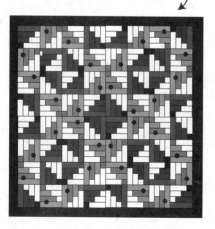

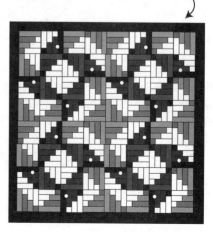

Arrangements for 16 Blocks with a V/H Pattern

Centers of these designs have the vertical/horizontal arrangements of seams shown here, just the opposite from those on page 123. You can add the borders on page 128 to these designs.

Center Unit Uses Regular Blocks

Center Unit Uses Reverse Blocks

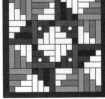

Remember, the blocks with the dots are Reverse blocks. I always show at least half of the blocks Regular. What if you have mostly Reverse blocks because you made a mistake, changed your mind, or are using leftovers? Switch the places of Reverse and Regular blocks and make a mirror image of a suitable design. As I have said many times, these designs are just to get you started. You can alter any of them as much as you please, changing colors, substituting plain blocks, taking parts of different designs and mixing them up, etc.

Anita's Sketchbook
Borders for 16-block V/H Designs— Lots of Dots

These borders were planned to go with 16-block designs on page 127. Putting vertical and horizontal seams in the opposite position, I got a high percentage of Reverse blocks, breaking my rule of at least half the blocks being Regular! I tried modifying them, then realized that since the best way to get nice corners for V/H designs was to use Reverse blocks, there wasn't much I could do. You may want to use these with center designs from page 48 (all Regular).

Already committed to a center from page 127? Choose a border with a star (mostly Regular), or switch to a border from page 49. (Or just break the "mostly Regular" rule and make mostly Reverse.)

Add More Borders, Keeping Reverse Blocks Balanced

As I mentioned, if you want to make a large quilt by adding borders on page 128, you might find the combination needs way too many Reverse blocks. Here are two ways to keep at least half Regular blocks:

Start with a 16-block design from page 127. Add a border with a star from page 128 to make 36 blocks.

Use the same general pattern for a second border, making 64 blocks.

Add an additional border to make 100 blocks. Count all of the Regular and Reverse blocks in one quadrant and multiply by four for the total.

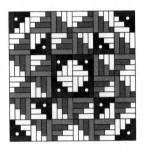 → 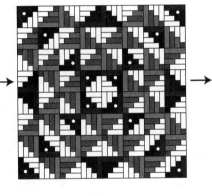 →

Start with a center from page 48 (all Regular blocks) and add a border from page 128 (heavy on Reverse blocks). When you add more borders, you'll probably find they are automatically balanced between Regular and Reverse.

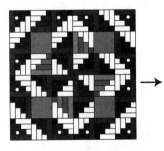 → 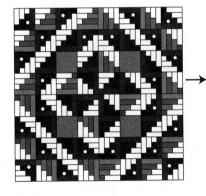 →

Remember, you can use plain squares anywhere they are needed to improve the design or make up for a shortage of pieced blocks.

More 16-block Designs Combined into 64-block Quilts

Here are some of my favorite ways to combine designs on page 127 into larger quilts. There were so many great possibilities that it was hard to just six. You can see that I favor designs with twirling Pinwheels.

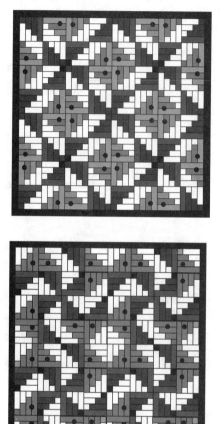

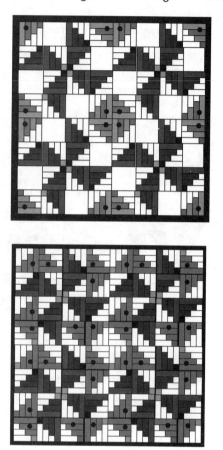

Notice that these bottom two are the same design. Blocks are rotated so darks and lights trade places, and other color changes are made. You can get quite a different look from many designs by adapting them like this:

Summary of Design Ideas

Earlier in the book I have had many Sketchbook pages devoted to designing your own quilts. Use this list to look back at pages you might have missed:

Part 1, Regular Blocks Only:

Overall designs, pages 41 to 43
Designs with Circle Centers (H/V)
- 16-block designs, page 44
- Borders that work with those designs, page 45 (interchangeable with pages 123 to 124)
- Adding more borders to those designs, page 46
- Combining those designs into 64-block quilts, page 47

Designs with Pinwheel Centers (V/H)
- 16-block designs, page 48
- Borders that work with those blocks, page 49 (Interchangeable with pages 127 and 128)
- Adding more borders to those designs, page 50
- Combining those designs into 64-block quilts, page 51
- More ideas for Pinwheel designs, pages 52

Table Runners, pages 59 and 60
Designing Large Quilts, pages 71 to 74

Part 2, Regular Plus Reverse Blocks:

Overall Designs, pages 114 and 115
Designs with H/V Centers
- 16-block designs, page 123
- Borders that work with those blocks, page 124 (interchangeable with pages 44 and 45)
- Adding more borders to those blocks, page 125
- Combining those ideas into 64-block quilts, page 126

Designs with V/H Centers 127
- 16-block designs, page 127
- Borders that work with those blocks, page 128 (interchangeable with pages 48 and 49)
- Adding more borders to those blocks, page 129
- Combining those ideas into 64-block quilts, page 130

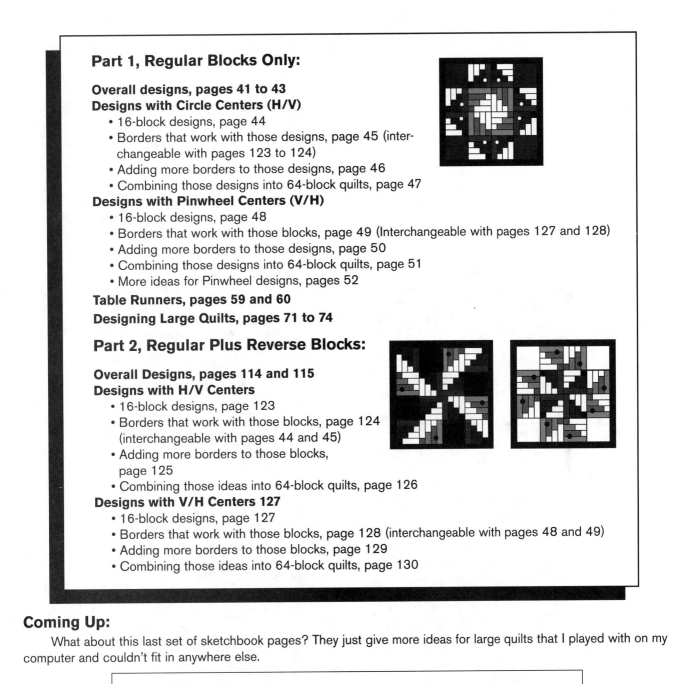

Coming Up:

What about this last set of sketchbook pages? They just give more ideas for large quilts that I played with on my computer and couldn't fit in anywhere else.

More Design Ideas
- Barn Burning (a special Straight Furrows/Barn Raising idea), page 127
- More Rotating Quadrants, page 133
- Simple changes, page 133
- Nice Things in the Center (medallion quilts), page 134
- Use Your Imagination (more creative touches), page 135

Anita's Sketchbook

Barn Burning

On pages 93, 95, and 97, I showed how to make Straight Furrows and showed how the idea was tied to Barn Raising.

Here's any easy way to add excitement to those basic designs:
- Make 64 blocks, 32 Regular and 32 Reverse, any size, preferably scrappy big blocks.
- Lay out 16 blocks as shown on page 93. Then rotate four blocks to change the pattern to this:
- Make three more sets of 16 blocks sewn together the same way (colors in the same positions, if you have distinct color schemes).
- Now combine the quilts into one. It's magic! Here are the new arrangements you can make.

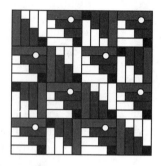

I don't need to remind you that you can add a layer or two of borders to whichever quilt you make. Use ideas from page 50.

More Rotating Quadrants

Same quadrants arranged another way:

20
16
8
16

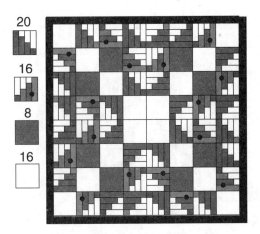

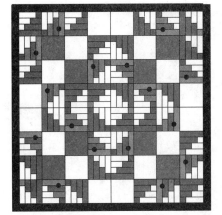

Simple Changes

Here's a nice pleasant 64-block arrangement, half Regular and half Reverse. If it's too ordinary, make creative changes. The possibilities are endless.

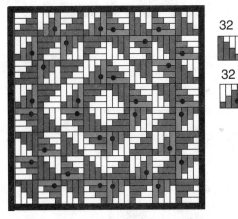

32

32

Here's the same layout, with plain blocks substituted and colors changed.

The same design, with a few blocks rotated and colors distributed a different way.

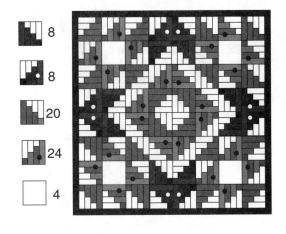

8
8
20
24
4

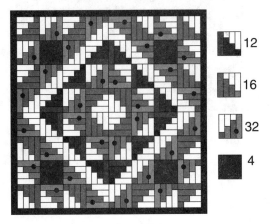

12
16
32
4

Nice Things in the Center

100 blocks

36

32

32

36

40

24

If you want to make a medallion quilt, or just frame a pretty panel of some sort as Gloria Pritchett did on page 89, adapt the outer sections of almost any large design. Here are the designs above with something else in the center.

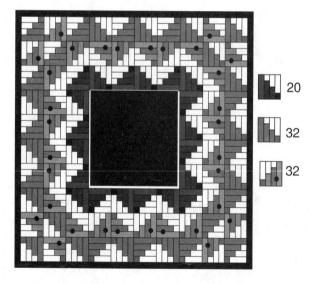

20

32

32

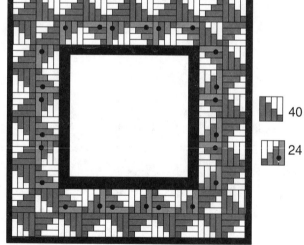

40

24

Also see the medallion quilt on page 107.

Anita's Sketchbook

Use Your Imagination

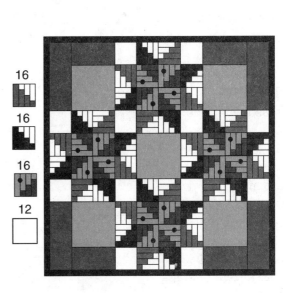

16

16

16

12

Right: Double or triple the design options by using some blocks which are dark and medium, as well as those which are distinctly dark and light. A few Woodpile blocks go a long way as the background space is broken up in a creative way. This design would probably be best on a small scale.

Below: Woodpile blocks repeat the Pinwheel design as they break into the border.

52

32

Below: This was modified from a 64-block quilt on page 130. (It had four repeats of a 16-block motif; this has almost nine repeats.) Colors gradually merge with each other in a hazy overall design of swirling shapes.

(Project 19, Cozy Quilt, continued from page 101)

5. Sew pairs together. Keep the largest Light area on top each time. Chain sections together like this:

6. Make 12 blocks.

a. Join sewn pairs to make a test block. Adjust seams to make it 5-1/2" wide.

b. Press toward the dark.

c. Trim ends so it is 5-1/2" square; the small square must be 1-1/2".

d. Adjust seams, if needed, and continue making blocks.

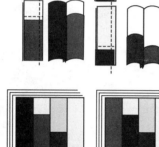

7. Make 12 more Regular blocks from the second color group. Follow Steps 3 to 6.

8. Make Reverse blocks. Follow Steps 3 to 7, with one big difference: For Step 5, turn over the stacks of cross-sections. This makes the steps go the other direction. Make 12 blocks from one color scheme, and 12 from the other. Continue to monitor seam width so blocks are exactly 5-1/2" wide. Leave blocks stacked neatly in four piles.

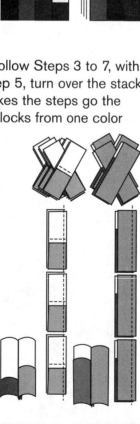

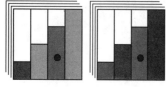

9. Following the directions on page 95, arrange blocks into

a. Barn Raising pattern.

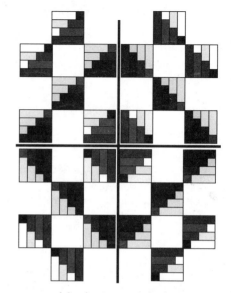

b. Rotate some blocks to match the pattern below. (If you find another pattern you like better, that's okay too.)

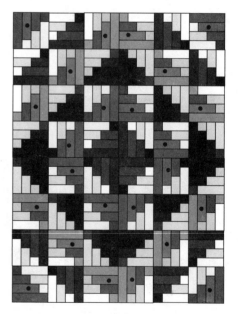

10. Add borders. Cut borders 4" wide, or any desired width. To avoid piecing the side borders, add borders to the sides first, then the ends. Marilyn mitered her corners. That is more attractive, but it requires side borders longer than 44", so you will need 1-1/4 yards of border fabric to avoid piecing.

11. Quilt and bind with your favorite method.

(Project 20, Boca Barn Raising, continued from page 102)

6. Complete a test block. Measure it to make sure it is 5-1/2" wide. Adjust seams if needed.

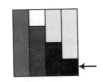

7. Complete the first 12 Regular blocks. Sew carefully so they are 5-1/2" wide. Trim the ends as shown on page 15, making sure the small Dark pieces (arrow) are exactly 1-1/2" square.

8. Make 12 Reverse blocks. Follow Steps 5 to 7, but turn all cross-sections over so those on top have larger sections of dark fabric.

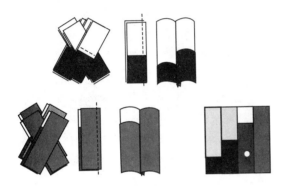

9. Repeat Steps 2 to 7 to make three more sets of blocks, 12 Regular and 12 Reverse each time. You'll be short a few blocks; make up the shortage in Step 11.

10. Do a trial arrangement. This is tricky; I hope you like puzzles. Look at page 95 and Zvia's quilt on page 102. Lay out the Regular blocks like this first, with yarn dividing the quilt into quadrants. Within each quadrant, blocks are all turned the same way **except** for the ones in the center. Some blocks are missing. Make them in Step 11.

---

11. Fill in the rest of the design. Here's one quadrant to get you started:

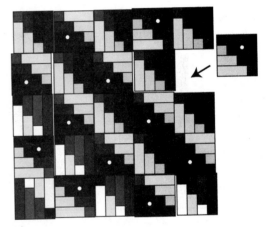

12. Make a few more blocks. Count how many more you need of each type. Do some quick strip piecing, repeating any fabrics you have already used (or using new ones). Use the same widths as in Step 1, but these lengths:
8" for four blocks
9" for five blocks
11" for six blocks

13. Make a final arrangement and sew the quilt together.

14. Add borders. Zvia used an inner border 1-1/2" wide and an outer border about 5" wide.

15. Quilt and bind with your favorite method.

4. Cut 1-3/4" cross-sections. You need 12 from each set, a total of 48 of each Dark/Light combination. If you can't get that many, cut a few individual

pieces from scraps and piece them together.

5. Sew sections together. Keeping the larger light sections on top, sew with scant 1/4" seams, chaining like this: Press pairs.

6. Assemble the blocks.

a. Make a test block.

b. Combine sections.

c. Add a long (E) strip.

d. Press, measure, and square up as shown on page 15. The block must be 6-3/4" square. The small Dark A square must be 1-1/2".

e. Make 48 blocks, mixing up parts for a scrappy look.

7. Make 16 Reverse blocks.

a. Repeat Steps 2 to 4.

b. Turn the stacks of sections over.

c. Sew with the larger dark sections on top. When opened, the pairs have a stepping-up pattern.

d. Assemble 16 blocks, keeping the seam width which makes blocks exactly 6-3/4" wide. Mix up parts for more variety if you wish. (That's not as important this time.)

e. Press and trim the blocks, again checking to make sure the small Dark A pieces are exactly 1-1/2" square.

8. Make 16-block units.

a. Assemble 16 blocks in the pattern below. Watch the small dark squares. They need to line up with seams in adjoining blocks, and they need color contrast with their neighbors (especially in the center of the Pinwheel).

b. Repeat the arrangement four times.

9. Add any borders you desire. Fabric allowances were for these widths:

Inner border 1-3/4" wide (cut five 44" strips)

Outer borders 5" wide (cut six 44" strips)

10. Quilt and bind with your favorite methods. Scrap quilts look fine commercially machine quilted with an overall pattern which doesn't follow the patchwork design.

(Project 22, Tulips in the Woodpile, continued from page 104)

2. Sew strips into panels. Pair off the 22" strips and sew them together like this: To avoid accidentally sewing the wrong strips together, pin them and see if the width of the two strips equals about

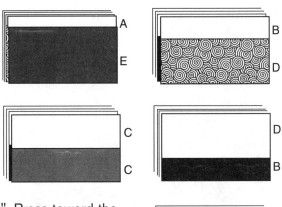

10". Press toward the darks.

3. Cut cross-sections. With panels stacked with right sides up, seams parallel but offset to reduce bulk, cut all layers into 2" sections, 10 stacks from each set.

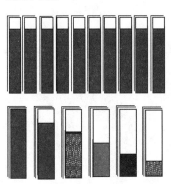

Stack each combination neatly, along with the 2" x 10" strips.

4. Begin assembling Regular blocks. Assemble strips in this order. Sew with the largest light areas on top each time to get this stepping-down effect. As always, make a test block to assure that your blocks are exactly 9-1/2" wide. Press toward the dark and trim the top and bottom of the blocks to square them up. The small dark squares must be exactly 1-3/4". See page 76 for ideas for keeping the stacks organized as you seek a pretty combination of colors each time. (If two blocks end up with the same fabrics, no one will notice.)

5. Make Reverse blocks. After making a large supply of Regular blocks, start making Reverse blocks. (This time, have the areas with the largest dark areas on top as you sew.)

6. Add to the stash. As you make one block after another, you will find yourself rejecting some sections and eagerly searching for more of your favorites. Go back to Step 1 and make more strips in colors that complement the rejects and fabrics that you enjoy working with the most.

7. Decide on your arrangement. After making about 24 Regular and 24 Reverse blocks, start laying them out. You're sewing for fun and it's okay to change your mind and switch to another design if you wish. (Make two smaller quilts, in fact.) When you decide on your design, finish making your blocks and sew them together.

8. Quilt and bind with your favorite methods. Diane's quilt has a beautiful combination of machine quilting in the dark areas and hand quilting—with a tulip motif—in the light areas.

(Project 23, Fireman's Fancy, continued from page 106)

4. Cut apart half of the sets.
a. Cut 24 cross-sections, 1-3/4" wide from one of each combination with Red strips. (If you can't get 24, cut replacement parts from scraps.)
b. Repeat with one of each type with Black strips.
c. Stack the sections like this: Keep the colors in the positions shown in the art.

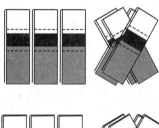

5. Make a test block.
a. Sew pairs together, lining up seams carefully.
b. Assemble the block. Ends will be uneven.
c. Press toward the darker side.
d. Adjust seams, if necessary, so the block is 5-1/2" wide. Use that exact seam width for future blocks.

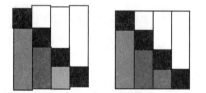

6. Assemble 48 Regular blocks. Make 24 blocks with Red squares and 24 with Black squares. Trim ends so they are 5-1/2" square.
7. Make 48 Reverse blocks.
a. Repeat Steps 4 to 6, turning over stacks so colors look like this:

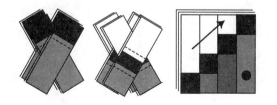

8. Cut 48 plain blocks from Background fabric.
a. Cut 24 pieces 5-1/2" x 10-1/2" of Fabric 1. (Cut six 5-1/2" x 44" strips, then divide each into four blocks.)
b. Cut 24 more pieces 5-1/2" x 10-1/2" from Fabric 2.
Alternative: Cut blocks from a variety of fabrics.

9. Assemble units like this,
using two different fabrics here:

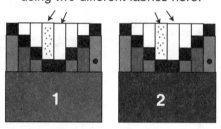

a. Sew each Regular block with Red squares to a Reverse block (dot) with Red squares.
b. Sew them to blocks from Background Fabric 1.
c. Sew all of the blocks with Black squares to each other the same way, then to blocks from background Fabric 2.
10. Join units into 12 larger units like this:

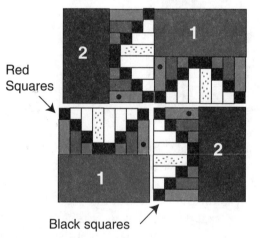

Red Squares

Black squares

11. Assemble the quilt top. Join the 12 units, matching the quilt on page 106.
12. Add borders. To match the quilt Teri made, cut eight strips 4" to 4-1/2" wide.
13. Quilt and bind with your favorite methods.

Cutting Directions for Project 24, Fanning the Fire (continued from page 109)

Lennie made her quilt with a large array of fabrics; I am simplifying for fat quarters. You can substitute scraps for any of these strips for a richer effect. (Calculations do not include pieced borders.)

General method:

Most fat quarters will be trimmed to 16" x 22", so you can cut 16" strips with a minimum of waste. (Save the trimmings—about 1-3/4" to 2" wide and 22" long—some will be needed.)

Blues fabrics

Use seven fat quarters.
Trim six of them to 16" wide.
Stack four fat quarters. Cut, four at a time:
- A = Eight strips 2" x 16"
- B = Eight strips 3-1/4" x 16"
- C = Four strips 4-1/2" x 16"
- D = Four strips 5-3/4" x 16"

Stack two more fat quarters. Cut:
- C = Four strips 4-1/2" x 16"
- D = Four strips 5-3/4" x 16"

Don't trim the seventh fat quarter; cut it the long way into six strips 1-3/4" x 22". Stack these strips and cut:
- E = 16 pieces 1-3/4" x 7*
- *Can be slightly shorter if fabric was skimpy.

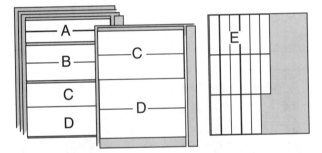

"Drab" fabrics (variegated blues, grays, browns)

Use two fat quarters.
Trim both to 16" wide. Stack and cut:
- a = Eight strips 1-3/4" x 16"
- A = Four strips 2" x 16"

Tip: If you don't have variegated fabrics with transitions from one color to another, use scraps of Blue or other fabrics for about half of these strips.

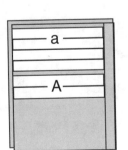

Red fabrics

Use six fat quarters.
Stack four fat quarters. Trim to 16" wide, then cut, four at a time:
- A = Four strips 2" x 16"
- B = Four strips 3-1/4" x 16"
- C = Four strips 4-1/2" x 16"
- D = Four strips 5-3/4" x 16"

Cut the fifth and sixth fat quarters, into 11 strips 1-3/4" x 22". Stack several at a time and cut them into smaller pieces:
- E = 32 pieces 1-3/4" x 7"*
- *Can be slightly shorter if fabric was skimpy.

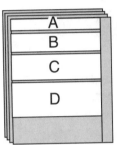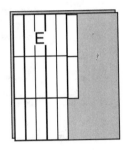

Light fabrics

Use three fat quarters.
Trim all to 16".
Stack two fat quarters. Cut, two at a time:
- A = Ten strips 2" x 16"
- B = Two strips 3-1/4" x 16"
- C = Two strips 4-1/2" x 16"

Cut from third fat quarter:
- D = Two strips 5-3/4" x 16"

Cut from scraps (remnants from above steps, 2" x 22" trimmings, or other Light scraps):
- a = Ten strips 1-3/4" x 16"

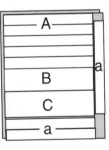

Step-by-step instructions for Fanning the Fire are continued on page 142.

Step-by-step instructions for Fanning the Fire are continued on page 142.

(Project 24, Fanning the Fire, continued from page 109)

7. Complete 48 blocks, following the basic steps on pages 13 to 15.

a. Make 32 Red/blue blocks

b. Make 16 Blue/Light blocks.

8. Sew strips together for Shattered blocks. Make two of each panel. Be really accurate and consistent now. You will have a lot of seams to line up in Step 10.

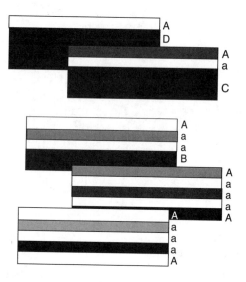

Design suggestion: Mix up the "Drab" colors in a different order in each panel. Have a big variety? Use the darker, cooler colors on the lower positions (closer to the blue), and use lighter, warmer colors in the higher positions.

9. Cut 1-3/4" cross sections. For accuracy, cut through only one layer at a time. You need eight from each. Try to get nine cross sections and choose the most accurate ones.

10. Assemble 16 blocks like this, lining up seams. Press and trim blocks on the lower end only.

11. Assemble the quilt top

a. Arrange four-block sets like this.

b. Arrange four sets at a time into 16-block units. (View it through a reducing glass or camera lens. You might prefer to arrange the blocks to emphasize the light pinwheels instead.)

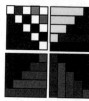

c. When you are satisfied with the arrangement, sew the body of the quilt together.

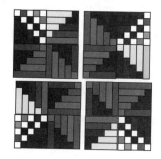

12. Add borders.

a. Cut five 1-3/4" x 44" strips of red and piece to fit for the inner borders.

Optional: Add pieced borders. My idea was that light squares would continue the swirling of the red pinwheels into the borders (arrows). If you agree, use leftover chains of squares from Step 10. Add dark strips long enough to connect one chain to the next (about 20"), and cut various lengths to fill in the corners. However, if the light pinwheels are the important part of the design, these squares might be a distraction, so don't use them.

b. Add outer borders. I like fairly wide borders to set the busy quilt off from its surroundings.

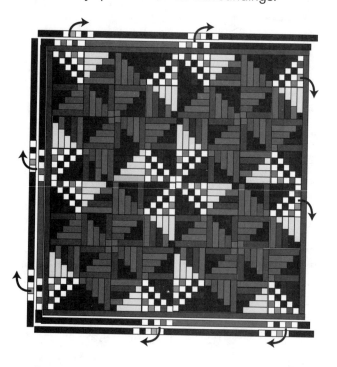

13. Quilt and bind as desired. Lennie used stippling. See the front cover.

(Project 25, Irish Cabin, continued from page 110)

3. Check for accuracy. Because you will have dozens of seams to line up, check before cutting apart to see that all of the narrow strips are exactly 1" wide—except those on the edges, which will be wider, of course, because the final seam hasn't been taken. Correct bad spots, or be prepared to discard sections. (You will have a couple of extra sections.)

4. Cut cross-sections. Cut 1-1/2" cross-sections, at least 12 sections from each pieced panel, eight from the solid panel. Instead of lining up panels and cutting through both layers, cut these cross-sections individually for greater accuracy. Check as you cut to make sure that the lines of the panels line up with the lines of your ruler.

5. Assemble six Regular blocks. The sections with more small squares will be on top each time as you sew. Use scant 1/4" seams. Discard or repair any sections where the seams don't line up. Check your first block to be sure it is exactly 6-1/2" wide. Press toward the dark side of the block. Make six blocks. Trim only one end to square up the blocks.

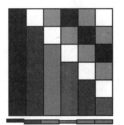

6. Assemble six Reverse blocks. This time the section on top as it goes through the machine will be the section with the largest pieces. Four blocks will not have an end strip.

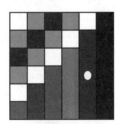

7. Make the center block. Use the template and directions on the following page. (You can substitute any other 6" to 8" appliqué or pieced block, of course.)

8. Assemble the wall hanging. Study these diagrams to see how the blocks go together. They do not follow a strict vertical-horizontal-vertical pattern as most Woodpile projects do.

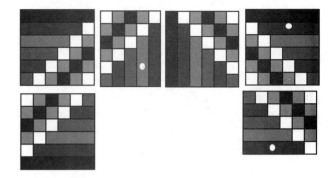

If you can't get seams to line up as accurately as you want, make a new block from leftovers. Or switch blocks around somewhat. Notice how the corner blocks are turned vertically below:

Combine the double blocks and the center unit first, then join the top and bottom blocks and add them.

9. Add borders of any width you like. An inner border 1-1/2" wide of Red or White would be nice. The outer border can be 3" or so.

10. Quilt and bind with your favorite methods.

Center of Irish Cabin Wall Hanging

a. Photocopy the Cabin diagram below, cut it apart and use the pieces as templates.

b. Cut out fabric (four or five colors), adding seam allowances, of course.

c. Assemble four main sections as shown at the right.

d. Join parts to make the Cabin.

e. Add white borders. Cut two 1-3/4" x 6" pieces for the sides and two 2" x 9-1/2" pieces for the top and bottom.

f. Add dark border. Cut 1-3/4" strips and add to each side. Trim to make it 11-1/2" square (or match the width of the double block in Step 8).

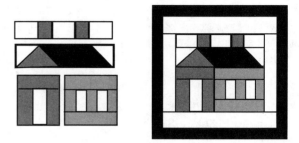

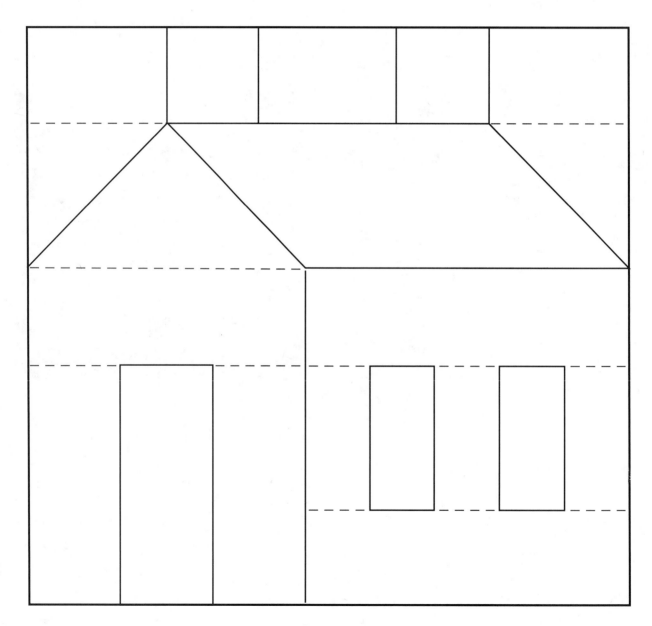

Appendix
An Illustrative Glossary

Block Characteristics

Standard:
Dark dominates

Alternate:
Light dominates

Design-Your-Own charts give both Standard and Alternate, but in the projects I have you use only

Slant:
Regular:

Reverse:

Standard blocks to avoid confusion.
Blocks in the first half of the book are all Regular. Projects in the second half are Regular plus Reverse blocks. See page 90 for how to make each type. (Reverse blocks have a dot in artwork.)

Scale: Width of sections after seams.
Mini: 3/4" **Small:** 1" **Normal:** 1-1/4" **Large:** 1-1/2"

Calculations are in the charts on pages 61 to 64. Most projects use Normal scale.

Steps

Most projects in this book use blocks with **four steps**. The chart on page 147 is a summary of the block scale and steps in all projects.

Seam directions

H/V   **V/H**

Keep seams in the **vertical** and **horizontal** position shown in the diagrams for the project you are doing. See pages 44, 48, 123, and 127 for uses of these two combinations in center motifs.

Center Motifs
Circles   Pinwheels

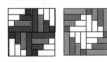

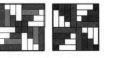

See the color photographs on pages 20 to 21. Page 131 has a guide to dozens of black and white designs built around each motif. On page 50 is a summary of the advantages of each motif if you are designing your own project.

"A" Square: The small square in the corner of each block. Exact size is important because seams often have to line up with the neighboring blocks.

Fat eighth: Piece of fabric about 11" x 18".

Fat quarter: Piece of fabric about 18" x 22".

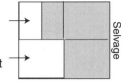

Log Cabin block: The most famous diagonally divided block. Log Cabin blocks are built up from the center, while Woodpile blocks are strip-pieced.

Log Cabin   **Woodpile**

Mock-up block: A diagram of the block. Paste on snippits of fabric to remember where fabrics will be used.

Quadrant: One-fourth of a quilt design; see page 134. Many quilts are formed by repeating the same motif four times.

Reducing glass: A lens to view tentative block layouts to see if you like the effect. By reducing the size you see the color and lines without the distraction of raw edges, etc. You can also look through a camera lens (or simply squint to blur the edges).

Peephole: Designed to install in a door, this is an inexpensive substitute for a reducing glass. Get one at your favorite hardware store.

Viewfinder: Two L-shaped pieces of paper or cardboard to help you adapt designs to your needs. Just cover part of the diagrams or photo to isolate the part you want to use. See page 42.

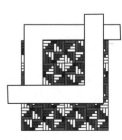

Coloring Sheets for Designing Your Own Quilt

I use a computer program to visualize special effects and color schemes, or I just start sewing and make it up as I go along. If you prefer to use colored pencils and plan quilts the old fashioned way, here are some 48-block outlines to get you started. (Photocopy, double up the art, and photocopy again for larger quilts.) I show the basic seam lines, but you'll have to provide the lines between dark and light pieces because there are so many different ways darks and lights can be positioned.

Four Steps

Three Steps

Six Steps

Five Steps

Sizes and Number of Steps in the Projects

Number of steps	Mini	Small	Normal	Large
2				5. Card Trick
3			10. Kelly's Sweetheart Quilt	11. Fancy Paths 12. Toasted Triangles
4 4 4 4 4	7. Seven Stars		1. Super Sixteen 2. Marcella's Quilt 3. Rain Dance 4. Christmas Table Runner 15. Kachina 19. Cozy Quilt 20. Boca Barn Raising 23. Fireman's Fancy	13. Housewarming 14. Glowing Pinwheels
5 5 5 5			6. Betsy's Pinwheels 8. Warm Hearts 21. Pinwheel Stars 24. Fanning the Fire	
6 6 6		16. Rainbow Hearts 25. Irish Cabin	18. Before and After	9. Log Cabin Look-alike 17. Barn-Raising 22. Tulips in the Woodpile

"Lemonade"–How to Salvage Bad Blocks

Problem 1: Blocks are not square

Solution 1: Add "piping" or "beading." Sew a 1" strip of striped fabric along either the side or end of the block . Then trim the block to be square. (If small squares won't line up with neighbors, look for arrangements where this won't be a problem.) Note: This piping will be offset in some arrangements, so consider that part of the design effect. This is a decorative touch you can add to blocks which are not defective. See the photo for Project 3. (If blocks are already wide enough, add only 3/4" strips, and put it between blocks so the design won't be offset.)

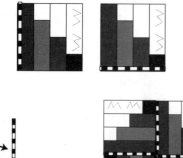

Solution 2: Alternate blocks with plain blocks. The best example is the Kachina quilt on page 91 because all blocks are vertical. Adapt this idea to the blocks you have. Instead of making "special" blocks, you can have a narrow sashing between blocks that would otherwise touch (see arrow).

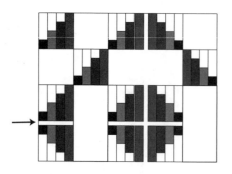

Solution 3: Use blocks in a border. See page 105 for examples. Put these borders around plain panels or other quilt tops, not around other Woodpile blocks since seams won't line up. Notice that all seams on each side go parallel to each other. If two blocks share end strips, there will be a lot of part blocks used. Caution: You have to plan carefully to have the design come out even. Even then, you might not be able to get a nice effect at the corners. It is easier to design the borders, then find or make a center panel to fit. One thing that is easy with these parallel seams is making the border slightly shorter by simply making wider seams here and there until it fits.

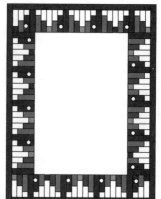

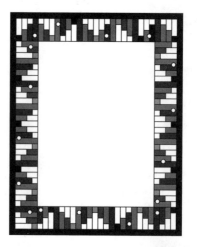

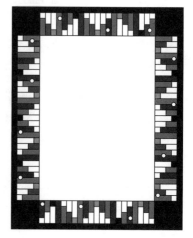

"Lemonade"—How to Salvage Bad Blocks

Problem 2: Blocks were sewn together wrong

Solution 1: Make the design a mirror image. If you were trying to make designs from the first half of the book (all Regular blocks) and found yourself accidentally sewing them together backwards, that's not fatal. If all blocks are the same, just use the design you started with, but mentally reverse the artwork or photo. If necessary, hold a small mirror up to the page.

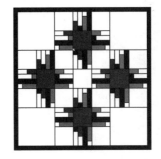

Solution 2: Change your mind. Your part blocks don't fit together? Make part-blocks they do fit with and switch to another design.

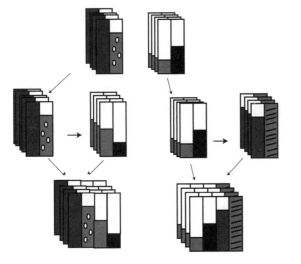

Solution 3: Work smaller. If a lot of blocks are messed up but you don't want to discard them, cut the seams clear off and assemble **smaller** blocks. Instead of lining up ends, monitor the height of the step (see page 15). Then trim the ends. (If you understand the Woodpile block enough to follow that, it probably wasn't you who goofed. You're probably trying to save blocks someone else ruined.)

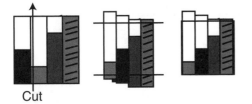

Cut

Solution 4: Use rejects in an imaginative way. If you have an occasional mistake, unsew it. But it's no fun to pick out a dozen seams or throw blocks away. It's worse if someone else goofs. (Maybe you are teaching children to sew, or non-quilters are helping with a special project.) Smile and make the best of it. Collect rejects for an "Art Quilt."

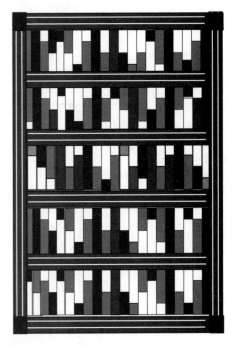

Calculating Curves

On page 112, I show blocks which create the illusion of being curved. The effect is created with unequal sections, of course. I don't have room to develop the idea (maybe it's the start of a future book). If you want to experiment on your own, here are some basic calculations:

Cut cross-sections: 1" 1-1/8" 1-1/4" 1-3/8" 1-1/2" 1-3/4"
Width after seams: 1/2" 5/8" 3/4" 7/8" 1" 1-1/4"

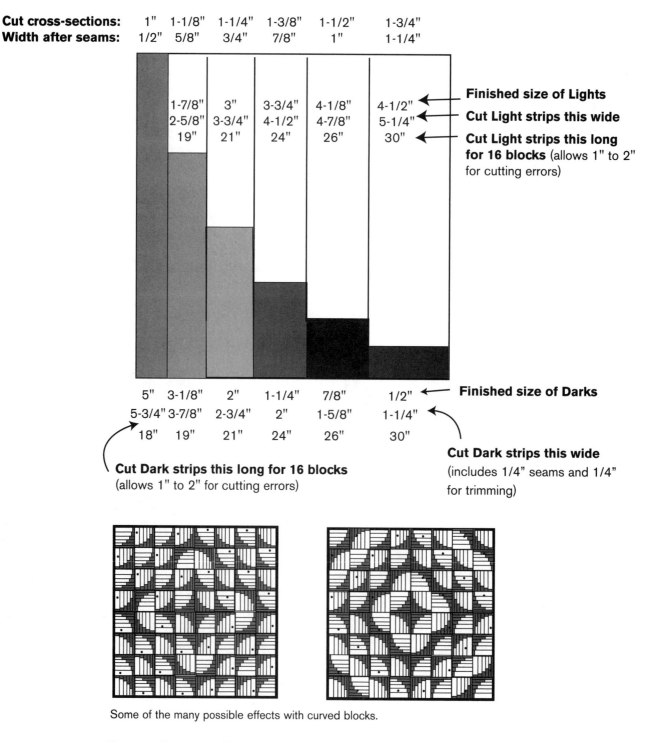

	1-7/8"	3"	3-3/4"	4-1/8"	4-1/2"	← **Finished size of Lights**
	2-5/8"	3-3/4"	4-1/2"	4-7/8"	5-1/4"	← **Cut Light strips this wide**
	19"	21"	24"	26"	30"	← **Cut Light strips this long for 16 blocks** (allows 1" to 2" for cutting errors)

5" 3-1/8" 2" 1-1/4" 7/8" 1/2" ← **Finished size of Darks**
5-3/4" 3-7/8" 2-3/4" 2" 1-5/8" 1-1/4"
18" 19" 21" 24" 26" 30"

Cut Dark strips this long for 16 blocks
(allows 1" to 2" for cutting errors)

Cut Dark strips this wide
(includes 1/4" seams and 1/4" for trimming)

Some of the many possible effects with curved blocks.

If you are intrigued with curves, please check my web page and contact me via e-mail. See page 157.

Help for Teachers

If you are a teacher, I invite you to teach Woodpile quilt classes at quilt guilds, stores, churches, recreation departments, community colleges, etc. The next few pages give some aids. For additional ideas, check my web page, send an e-mail to hallock@pacinfo.com, or send a self-addressed stamped envelope to P.O. Box 2, Springfield, OR 97477.

A Good Beginner's Class

I suggest you start with Project 1 with one change: Use two color schemes, making eight blocks of each. This will help students try more arrangements and understand some of the other projects. Contact me for a class announcement, supply list, and class handout you can legally photocopy.

On the following pages are instructions for making kits, which I suggest you do. Make more kits than you think you will need because some people will want to expand their projects to 24 or 32 blocks.

Use only Regular blocks for a simple beginner's class. If any students goof and sew blocks together in the Reverse pattern, have them try layouts using Reverse blocks. (They'll need four, eight, 12, or all 16 Reverse blocks.) Remember they can add or substitute plain blocks as needed.

Buddy System

Those who teach in small rooms will be glad to know that this beginner project works well for two friends sharing a sewing machine and other tools. One person can be cutting and pressing while the other is sewing.

Special Supplies for the Teacher

In addition to the supplies listed at the first of the book, you will find these supplies useful:
• A quilt visualizer, such as a reducing glass from a quilt shop, a camera lens, or a simple door peep-hole from a hardware store. These can be added to the supply list, if that suits your group.
• Striped fabric which is compatible with your kits and can be used to correct blocks which are too narrow (see page 148).
• 6" grids to square up the blocks, unless you are sure students will have their own.
• Flannel boards or other aids to display quilt parts to show the work in progress.
• A set of overlays (below)

Mock-up Blocks

On page 147 is the master copy of the four-step mock-up sheet I use for classes. I sometimes cut the sheet into thirds, giving students one copy to use for reference and the other to actually paste fabric to.

On page 148 is a second type of mock-up block master copy that can be used when students are making Regular and Reverse blocks from different color schemes. Make a copy of the whole sheet for each person. (On page 12 are diagrams for the other sizes, not just four steps.)

Try to have students make their own mock-up blocks, using snippets from the 1/2" wide strips of every fabric that you cut while making the kits (see page 153). This step isn't too important this time since the fabrics in the kits are already lined out to show how the block will look. But having them do it in class enforces the idea that they should make mock up blocks when they do projects on their own.

In a large class, making mock-up blocks might not be workable if everyone is trying to find all the snippets at one time. (When you make the kits, you could cut snippets of every fabric for each kit, put them in a baggie and add them to the kits, but this might take more time than you are willing to spend.)

Experimenting with Different Block Layouts

Once students finish their 16 blocks, I encourage them to try different arrangements. You might photocopy pages 44 and 48, cut the sheets apart, and put one sketch in each kit. Ask the students to try that one and let the class see it before deciding on the one they want to actually use.

Expanding Projects

Some students in each class will probably want to expand their 16 blocks to a larger quilt. Have several extra kits available so they can buy additional ones.

It's nice to have a classroom set of four transparent overlays (laminated photocopies of the borders on pages 45, 49, 124, and 128 with transparent windows). Help them visualize the 16-block arrangements with various borders added. I may make these available for sale; check my web page (see page 157).

Should the Teacher Make Kits?
Advantages of Kits:
• Students can begin sewing immediately; there's no waiting for you to help them choose fabrics.
• There's room for more students since only small cutting mats are needed.
• Students like kits; they come relaxed instead of being worried about whether they chose the right fabrics. Although you need to charge for your time, kits are still a bargain because they don't have to buy a lot of fabric, use a little and have a lot of leftovers.
• Most important: Students are more likely to be pleased with the results. It takes experience—or several sample quilts and printed guidelines (such as a copy of this book) to study ahead of time—to choose the right fabrics for Woodpile quilts.

Disadvantages:
• It takes time to make up the kits.
• Some students want unique fabrics, not the same color scheme used by someone else.
• If students want more of a certain fabric for borders or plain blocks, the fabric might not be available.

The Winner: Make Kits
I make kits for 16 blocks in two color schemes in four steps, Normal size (the block used for Projects 1, 2, 3, 15, 19, and 20). If class time will be short, I even sew the strips together in pairs. (They work up fast with a serger, and handling and packing bags is easier.)

The Disadvantages Disappear:
Time: You can charge for the time spent prewashing, cutting, and packing kits. I basically double the cost of the fabric, and everyone thinks that's fair. Although I spent many hours the first time I made up kits, you'll find it quick if you cut and organize as I show you.
Individuality: The kits I describe have variety built in. No two projects will be alike. I have extra strips that can be traded. Really confident and creative people aren't as likely to be in a beginner class; they'll teach themselves from the book I give students the option of bringing lots of scraps of their own fabrics and coming early. Few students will opt to do that, but those who do will find it easier to select fabrics on their own before class as they look at the kits you brought.
Matching fabric: If you teach at a shop or buy fabrics at an easily accessible local shop, this isn't a problem. If you are coming in from the outside, bring some extra of some of the fabrics. (Be aware that borders and other quilt parts don't need to be an exact match.)

A 16-block kit should contain:
• Mock up diagrams
• Two packets of strips, each making eight blocks, four steps, Normal size
• A diagram for arranging 16 blocks (there are many different ones, so other students around them will have different versions).

Supplies for 20 (or more) kits, plus spare parts:
Study pages 10, 11, and 18 before buying fabric.

• Dark fat quarters: 34
• Light fat quarters: 19
• Yardage?

Make all of the fabric somewhat coordinated for simplicity.

Yardage? You might also choose to have yardage for borders and plain blocks; I suggest that you use the B fabrics.
• Bags: A box of 50 food storage bags at least 6" x 6-1/2"
• Safety pins to pair off two bags at a time.
• Storage for snippits, extra strips, and spare parts. Try shallow boxes or trays, gallon food storage bags, and maybe a loose leaf notebook with heavy duty sheet protectors.

I pack eight-block kits in plastic bags, with each fabric folded over to resemble the finished block.

For a large class, choose two compatible eight-block sets and clip or pin them together to make one 16-block set. Have students make up one set before opening the other bag to minimize the number of strips they have to organize at once. Allow students to trade the second eight-block set for a different one—after they understand the block and see the need to have contrasts among all Dark A and end strips.

Making 20 (or more) Kits

You'll need to cut these types of strips:
• Regular strips, 15" long, usual widths, 14 per kit, plus some extras for the "trade box."
• "Spare parts" to replace any parts damaged by errors or to make a few more blocks for alternative arrangements.

General Technique

1. Wash and press fat quarters as needed. I like to use spray starch.

2. Trim off excessive printed selvages (over 3/8" wide).

3. Stack as many fat quarters as you are comfortable with, two edges aligned. Trim and square up those edges.

4. Measure 15" and cut off surplus along one long edge. Fold over the stack of remnants and pin or clip them together to keep them neat for "spare parts."

5. Cut strips as directed below for the kits. Cut smaller strips from remnants.

Cut 15" strips for kits.

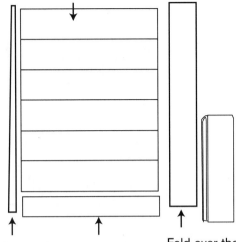

Cut 1/2" x 10" strips for mock-up blocks.

Cut more A strips from remnants.

Fold over the stack of 3" remnants; keep for "spare parts."

A strips:
Stack three dark fat quarters, all small prints, all contrasting with each other, but all coordinated. Cut 10 (or 11) strips 2" x 15" from each stack. Repeat with three light fat quarters.

B strips:
Stack five dark fat quarters, all coordinated to be interchangeable. Cut six strips 3-1/4" x 15" from each pile. Repeat with five light fat quarters.

C strips:
Choose 11 dark fat quarters, all coordinated to be interchangeable. Stack as many layers at a time as you are comfortable with. Cut four strips 4-1/2" x 15" from each stack. Repeat with 11 light fat quarters.

D strips:
Stack 15 dark fat quarters, all coordinated but with as much contrast as possible. Stack as many layers at a time as you are comfortable with. Cut three stacks 6" x 15" from each pile. (No light fabric is needed.)

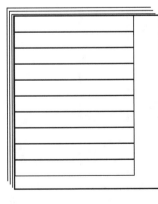

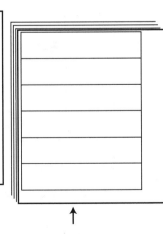

Cut extra A strips from remnants

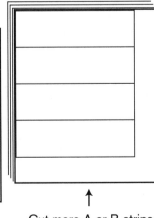

Cut more A or B strips from remnants.

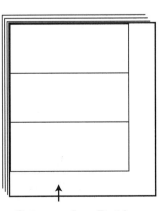

Cut more A or B strips from remnants.

Mock-up Blocks (Paste on 1/2" snippits with Glue Stick)

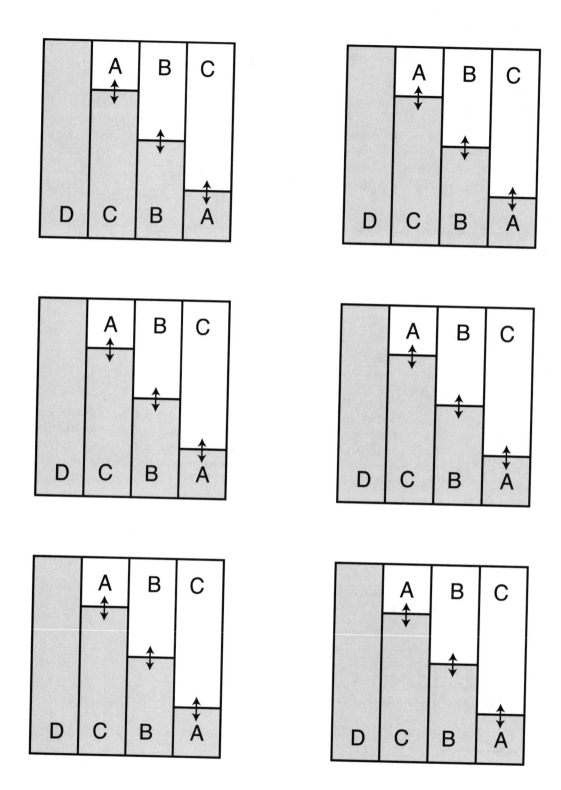

Mock-up blocks for quilts with both Regular and Reverse blocks

To visualize your blocks, paste 3/4" snippits of fabric to these diagrams with Glue Stick.

Regular

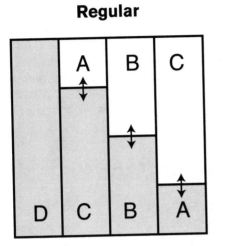

Reverse

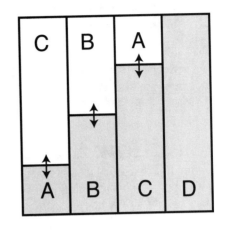

Keep these diagrams for reference.

Regular

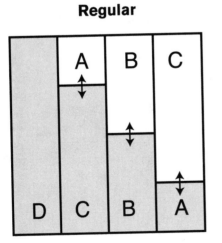

Reverse

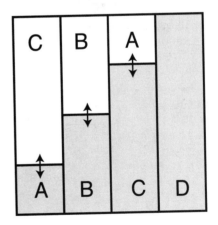

Quilts on the Covers

Front cover:
The background quilt is a detail of Fanning the Fire (Project 24 on page 109), made by Lennie Honcoop of Elk Grove, California.

The smaller quilt, "Bonfire," was made by Anita Hallock and Betty Hawkins. See instructions below.

Back cover:
The large quilt is Kachina (Project 15 on page 91), made by Cindy Fuelling, of Fredonia, Arizona. She expanded the quilt with pieced borders, added Prairie Points around the edges, and quilted the project by hand.

The Irish Cabin wall hanging (Project 25 on page 110) was one of two similar quilts made by Betsy Heath of Cheshire, Massachusetts. She made two sets of blocks, one featuring red fabrics, the other blues and greens. The squares were the same in both sets. This quilt, commissioned as a gift for a retiring schoolteacher, Pat Morandi, has four red blocks and eight blue ones. The second quilt uses eight red blocks and four blue ones.

How the Bonfire Quilt Was Made

At our 1999 retreat, I shared my ideas for a cover quilt coordinated with Lennie's background quilt. Betty Hawkins of Gig Harbor, Washington, pieced the inside and the black border with gold triangles, then ran out of time, so I took it home to finish it. I wanted wide dark blue borders to separate the two busy designs, but plain borders didn't look good, so I added a border of 20 red and blue blocks as a transition. I liked the effect and wished I had thought of it sooner (before we used the last bit of some of the red fabrics).

Calculations for Bonfire are somewhat complicated. Only the 16 inside blocks are complete. The outer blocks are only three-quarters as wide or tall as usual because parts of them are visually "behind" the black border. Note: Use the red fabrics in the same positions in the inner and outer blocks; don't try to match the sample.

16 Inner blocks:

Red fabrics	Light fabrics
A = 2" x 33"	2" x 33"
B = 3-1/2" x 33"	3-1/2" x 33"
C = 5" x 33"	5" x 33"
D = 6-1/2" x 33"	

Outer blocks:
Twelve 3/4 wide blocks

Red fabrics	Blue fabrics
A = 2" x 25"	2" x 25"
B = 3-1/2" x 25"	3-1/2" x 25"
C = 5" x 25"	5" x 25"

D strips are not used, except for four pieces 5" x 2" in the corners

Eight 3/4 tall blocks
Use the same A, B, C, and D fabrics as above, but make Red strips 2" narrower. (Blues are normal widths.)

Red fabrics	Blue fabrics
A = (not used)	2" x 17"
B = 2" x 17"	3-1/2" x 17"
C = 3-1/2" x 17"	5" x 17"
D = 5" x 17"	

Triangles:
Cut 36 squares, 2" wide of gold fabric.

Basic quilt assembly is similar to Project 13 on page 39. I'll try to put a color diagram for making this quilt on my web page.

Related Books

Fanning, Robbie and Tony. *The Complete Book of Machine Quilting, 2nd Edition*. Iola, WI: Krause Publications, 1994.

Hallock, Anita. *Fast Patch: A Treasury of Strip-Quilt Projects*. Iola, WI: Krause Publications, 1989.

Hallock, Anita and Betsy Hallock Heath. *Fast Patch Kids' Quilts: Dozens of Designs to Make for and with Kids*. Iola, WI: Krause Publications, 1996.

Hallock, Anita. *Scrap Quilts Using Fast Patch*. (Out of print. Copies are available from Anita Hallock, P.O. Box 2, Springfield, OR 97477.)

Wagner, Debra. *Traditional Quilts, Today's Techniques*. Iola, WI: Krause Publications, 1997.

Information on the Web

Information available on Anita's web page:
www.pacinfo.com/~hallock:
- More information about the quilts on the covers
- Tips for teachers (making kits, etc.)
- Answers to reader questions (send questions to Anita by e-mail at hallock@pacinfo.com)
- Notices of any errors
- How projects got their ratings (page 6)

Also check http://2204.249.244.10/Errata.htlm, a web site devoted especially to errors in various quilt books and magazine articles.

Index

A

Accuracy, 15
Adventures with 100 blocks, 97
Alignment of "A" squares, 15-16, 147
Alternate blocks, 32, 62-64, 145
Anita's Sketchbook, summary of design topics, 131
Autographs on friendship quilts, 79

B

Bachelor's Puzzle, 107
Barn Burning, 132
Barn Raising
    How to arrange blocks, 95, 97
    On point, 98
    Project 17, 96
    Varying basic arrangement, 99, 101
Before and After, Project 18, 98
Betsy's Pinwheels, Project 6, 29
Block arrangements, effect of Regular and Reverse, 113
Block sizes, charts, 61-64
Boca Barn Raising, Project 20, 102
Bodine, Joanne, 38
Borders, 16
Borders of blocks
    Around a central panel, 89
    For H/V designs, Regular blocks, 45-46
    For H/V designs, Regular plus Reverse blocks, 124
    For V/H designs, Regular blocks, 49-50
    For V/H designs, Regular plus Reverse blocks, 128-129
    From double blocks, 105
    From Heart blocks, 67
    Multiple, for medallion quilts, 134

C

Card Trick, Project 5, 27
Carmichael, Helen, 18
Charts, blocks of different sizes, 61-64
    Lengths of Strips Needed, 65
    Stitch and Flip Triangles, four steps, 88
    Stitch and Flip Triangles, three steps, 87
Christmas quilt, 26
Christmas Table Runner, Project 4, 25
Circle and Pinwheel Balance Sheet, 50
Circle motif in center, Regular blocks only, 19, 44-47
Circle motif in center, Regular and Reverse blocks, 99, 123, 127
Clark, Doreen, 111
Coloring schemes, 11
Coloring Sheets, 146
Constructions of blocks, 9-15, 19
Cozy Quilt, Project 19, 101
Cross-sections, cutting and sewing, 14
Curve illusion, 112, 150
Cutting strips, 13

D

Deevy Carolyn, 108
Delostrinos, Celeste, 112
Design effects of Regular and Reverse blocks, 113
Designs, Circle based, Regular blocks, 44-47
Designs, Overall, Regular blocks only, 41-43
Designs, Pinwheel based, Regular blocks only, 48
Difficulty, ranking of projects, 6, 147
Directional designs, 10, 13
Double blocks, 105, 106

E

Erlandson, Muriel, 17
Expanding quilts with borders of blocks, 46, 49-50, 52, 124, 128-129

F

Fabric, 10-11, 18
Fancy Path, Project 11, 35-36
Fanning the Fire, Project 24, 109
Fireman's Fancy, Project 23, 106
Five-step chart, 63
Foisy, Nancy, 110
Four-step chart, 62
Friendship Quilt group project, 78-79
Fuelling, Cindy, 156, back cover

G

Glowing Pinwheels, Project 14, 40
Grzeskowiak, Susan, 35

H

H/V designs, 44, 123
Harris, Cynthia, 111
Harter, Teri, 106
Hawkins, Betty, 40, 156
Hearts, alternate to Card Trick, 67
Heath, Betsy, 3, 17, 29, 89, 156, back cover
Honcoop, Lennie, 109, 156
Housewarming, Project 13, 39

I

Irish Cabin, Project 25, 110

K

Kachina
    Project 15, 91
    Variations, 89, 92
Kamon, Christine, 35, 91
Kelly's Sweetheart Quilt, 10, 34

L

Large quilt ideas
    Regular Blocks only, 71-74
    Regular plus Reverse, 107, 135
Leighton, Diane, 104
Lemonade (correcting bad blocks), 148-149
Length of Strips, chart, 65
Log Cabin Look-alike, Project 9, 33
"Long arms," avoiding, 16

M

Marcella's Quilt, Project 2, 23
Marilyn's Quilt, 107, 134
Mennis, Pam, 17, 36, 110
Mistakes
    Ignoring, 111
    Repairing, 148-149
Mock-up blocks
    Why needed, 11, 18, 151
    Master copy, 12, 154, 155
    For Stitch and Flip Triangles, 87-88
Monbaron, Marcella, 21

O

Olson, Mimi Vang, 108
Overall designs
    Using Regular blocks, 41-43
    Using Regular blocks, plus Reverse blocks, 114-115

P

Pinwheel motif
    Regular blocks only, 20, 24, 48-54
    Regular plus Reverse blocks, 99, 106, 123, 126-127
Pinwheel Stars, Project 21, 103
Primitive Hearts, 67
Pritchett, Gloria, 89
Projects, ranked by ease of construction, 6

Q

Quadrants, repeating to make designs, 21, 23, 47, 51, 97, 100, 103, 109, 126, 130, 132-133
Quilt top; avoiding design problems, 16
Quilting, 16

R

Rain Dance, Project 3, 24
Rainbow Hearts, Project 16, 94
Regular blocks, how to make, 9-15, 19
Reverse blocks
    How to make, 90
    Design effects, 89, 113
Rohwedder, Laura, 31
Roland, Ann, 17
Roland, Marilyn, 101

S

Sanford, Lois, 111

Scrap quilts, 26, 32-34, 61-64, 75-76, 93, 96-98, 102-104
Scrap Quilts Using Fast Patch, 33, 98, 107
Serger, 10, 14
Setting on point, 27, 52-53, 98, 107-108
Seven Stars, Project 7, 30
Shattered Blocks, 108-110
Shephard, Elaine, 105
Six-step chart, 64
16-block designs
    Regular blocks only, 19, 22, 44, 48
    Regular plus Reverse, 123, 127
64-block designs, made by combining 16-block projects, 21, 23, 47, 51, 100, 126, 130, 132
Size of quilts, summary, 6
Sizes of blocks
    Charts for designing your own, 61-64
    Used in projects, list, 147
Smith, Jan, 105
"Spines," avoiding, 16
Squaring up blocks, 15
Stitch and Flip Triangles
    Charts, 87-88
    How to make, 35-40
Stoltenberg, Lois, 39, 90
Strahilevitz-Klein, Zvia, 102
Straight Furrows, 93-94, 97, 132
Super Sixteen, Project 1, 22
Supplies, 10
"Swastikas," avoiding, 16

T

Table runners, 25, 59-60
Teaching Woodpile classes, 151-155
Test blocks, 14
Test Pilots, 8
Three-step Chart, 61
Tischler, Nan, 92
Toasted Triangles, Project 12, 38
Tools and supplies, 10
Trimming blocks, 15
Tulips in the Woodpile, Project 22, 104

V

V/H designs, 48, 127
Visualizing designs
    By turning blocks wrong side up, 97
    With paper "L" viewfinder, 42
    With reducing glass, 145
    With laminated photocopies, 41, 45, 49, 124, 128, 151

W

Warm Hearts, Project 8, 31
Williams, Christine, 35

Z

Zimlich, Susan, 22